Fly Fishing Central & Southeastern Oregon

A No Nonsense Guide to Top Waters

Harry Teel

Rainbow over the Deschutes River canyon. Photo by John Judy.

Fly Fishing
Central & Southeastern Oregon

A No Nonsense Guide to Top Waters
ISBN 1-892469-09-X

Published by:
No Nonsense Fly Fishing Guidebooks
P.O. Box 91858
Tucson, AZ 85752-1858
(520) 547-2462
www.nononsenseguides.com

Printed in China

Editors: David Banks, Helen Condon, Howard Fisher
Maps, Illustrations, Design & Production: Pete Chadwell, Dynamic Arts
Front Cover Photo by Brian O'Keefe
Back Cover Photo by John Judy

About the Cover

An angler patiently fishes the crystal-clear waters of the Fall River. Big brown and rainbow trout make good use of the cover provided them by the numerous deadfalls and undercuts along this pristine central Oregon spring creek. The slow, slick water and large fish present a challenge even to skilled fly fishers. Photo by Brian O'Keefe.

The No Nonsense Creed

The best way to go fly fishing is to find out a little something about a water, then just go there. Experimentation, trial-and-error, wrong turns, surprises, self-reliance, and new discoveries, even in familiar waters, are what make the memories. The next best way is to learn enough from a local to save you from going too far wrong. You still find the water on your own, and it still feels as if you were the first to do so.

This is the idea for our unique No Nonsense fly fishing series. Our books reveal little hush-hush information, yet they give all you need to find what will become your own secret places.

Painstakingly pared down, our writing is elegantly simple. Each title offers a local fly fishing expert's candid tour of his or her favorite fly fishing waters. Nothing is oversold or out of proportion. Everything is authentic, especially the discoveries and experiences you get after using our books. In his outstanding book *Jerusalem Creek,* Ted Leeson echoes our idea: "Discovering a new trout stream is a wonderful thing, and even if its whereabouts are common knowledge, to come upon the place yourself for the first time is nonetheless true discovery."

No Nonsense Fly Fishing Guidebooks give you a quick, clear understanding of the essential information for fly fishing a region's most outstanding waters. The authors are highly experienced and qualified local fly fishers. The maps are tidied versions of the author's sketches.

Dedication

I dedicate this guide to my wife, Delores, and my five children, Brad, Bruce, Susan, Brett, and Shelley. Under duress at times, they've accompanied me on numerous fishing excursions.

I also dedicate this guide to my many fishing friends. They have taught me the fine points of reading water, casting, and selecting flies; the necessity of good equipment; and how to camp in perfect misery on a beautiful, warm summer day.

Author Harry Teel in Argentina.
Photo by Brad Teel.

Table of Contents

Photo by Pete Chadwell.

Photo by Pete Chadwell.

Photo by Eric Dunne.

Photo by John Judy.

Photo by Pete Chadwell.

Hunting big brookies and landlocked Atlantic salmon at Hosmer Lake. Photo by Brian O'Keefe.

FLY FISHING
ONLY

Acknowledgments

In 1998, for the revised edition, people suggested I include new waters in this book. Some I've not fished but I know to be of merit. I asked Jeff Perin, owner of The Fly Fisher's Place in Sisters, Oregon, if he would be kind enough to research these areas for inclusion in the guidebook. Jeff's name is noted in sections where he provided input and updated information. His valuable contributions to this edition include new lakes, charts, and information on steelhead fishing on the lower Deschutes.

The original No Nonsense author, Harry Teel. Photo by David Banks.

Contributor Jeff Perin on the Lower Deschutes with a beautiful Deschutes redside. Photo by Matt Klee.

One of Oregon's excellent spring creek fisheries, the Fall River. Photo by Pete Chadwell.

Foreword

You are holding the updated, newly designed, and most current edition of the first book in the No Nonsense Fly Fishing Guidebooks series. More important, the information and ideas here are the sum of a devoted angler's 65-plus years of experience fly fishing his home state. Harry Teel's direction is very valuable if you want to fly fish or explore our stomping grounds here in central and southeastern Oregon.

The way this book came about is worthy of note. At the onset of his second retirement from a "real" job, Oregonian Harry Teel decided to leave information for his children regarding fly fishing in Oregon. His second job, by the way, was starting and operating The Fly Fisher's Place, a fly shop in Sisters, Oregon. This is where many of us enjoyed learning fly fishing, were pointed in the right direction, and dropped a bundle: the essence of a great fly shop.

But back to the book. Mr. Teel then wrote down all his firsthand knowledge of Oregon fly fishing, acquired as an angler and outfitter. He even drew and annotated maps showing where to fly fish these waters. Dee, Harry's wife, fly shop partner, and angling companion, carefully organized Harry's thoughts and entered everything into their new home computer.

In 1992 my then neighbor (and friend) Harry was asked by close friends if they could get a copy when the book was completed. Harry then contacted me and asked if I would like to make a book out of his manuscript and drawings. I found that Harry's Marine Corps training and his education and career as an engineer came through in his manuscript. It had precision, parsimony, and a nuts-and-bolts approach to a hobby that is often portrayed and perceived as complicated. I remarked that the approach was a lot like him: no nonsense. Then, as they say, a brand was born.

At that time, there wasn't a fly fishing guidebook to our area. Over time, and thanks (very much) to our devoted readers, this book became popular. It has been reprinted five times. The fourth printing was a new edition, updated and with new waters highlighted by Jeff Perin, the present owner of The Fly Fisher's Place.

Now, as central Oregon has grown, the region has become something of a Northwest fly fishing focal point. Oregon has *tons* of great fishing waters, but the central and southeastern part of the state, Harry's old turf, seems the most amenable to our hobby. Please use and enjoy this guidebook and tread lightly on our territory. I *know* you'll enjoy finding out what Harry wrote down those many years ago. Give him some thanks next time you see him.

David Banks

Preface

I am very fortunate in many ways. In relation to fly fishing, I'm fortunate that I was born in Oregon, and that my father and his friends introduced me to fly fishing at a very early age. These circumstances allowed me to pursue trout, steelhead, and salmon fishing nearly continuously for the better part of 65 years.

Fly fishing has been an important part of these 65-plus years, as both a form of recreation and a business. There have been only two interruptions in my quest for full-time fishing. The first was my tour of duty in the South Pacific and China with the Marine Corp during World War II. The second was working for 30 years with CH2M Hill, Engineers. The latter was much more enjoyable than my first diversion from fly fishing. It also enabled me to support my wife and five robin-mouthed offspring. These years also provided me the opportunity to work in close association with the finest professional and technical people in engineering.

After retiring from CH2M Hill, and finding retirement somewhat boring, I opened The Fly Fisher's Place, a fly shop in the central Oregon town of Sisters. Running the shop was a most interesting, enjoyable, and rewarding experience. It allowed me to meet hundreds of wonderful people, fish with new friends, travel, explore fishing opportunities in other locations, and fulfill my lifelong dream of being involved in fly fishing on a full-time basis. I've also been able to record my fly fishing adventures in Oregon and now, through this guidebook, can offer you the benefit of these years of fly fishing and note taking.

The central and southeast regions of Oregon, (the high desert region) are the origins of some of the most beautiful and pristine lakes and streams to be found anywhere in the world. Each region has its own distinct character and splendor. Old-growth forests of pine and fir bound some waters, while ancient junipers and desert vegetation surround others.

It is at times difficult to keep your concentration on casting your fly to a rising trout when the vistas beyond your quarry are the snow-covered peaks of the Cascade Mountains, the desert's wonderful rim rock canyons, or the sheer magnitude of Steens Mountain. The scenery is a photographer's dream and a fly angler's haven.

The central and southeast regions also offer many opportunities for solitude. In most areas a short walk will take you into territory that is nearly undisturbed by human endeavors. Taking a break in the high desert country is a wonderful way to relax and rejuvenate your mind and body.

I believe you'll enjoy the fly fishing in this magnificent part of Oregon. More important, I think your fly fishing experiences in this area will always occupy a special place in your memory.

Harry Teel

Fly Fishing Central & Southeastern Oregon

My first fishing trip in central Oregon was with my father in 1933. At that time we lived in Milwaukie, Oregon, which is south of Portland. One day we visited a neighbor, who showed us some large rainbow trout he'd recently caught in the Deschutes River. The image is still vivid, even though this happened some 75 years ago when I was a boy of six. The following Sunday, Dad got me up at 3:00 a.m.. We jumped in the pickup and headed for Maupin, a small community on the banks of the Deschutes about 100 miles east of home. I followed Dad up and down the river that day. When he hooked a fish, he'd let me land it, or at least try to. We didn't end up with the number or size of trout we'd seen at our neighbor's, but it was a memorable day. It provided me with a lasting memory of Dad, and it was the day that started my continuing love for the Deschutes River and the central and southeast regions of Oregon.

Since that first experience on the Deschutes River, I've fished the high desert regions of Oregon hundreds of times. I've also had the good fortune to have fly fished from Argentina to Alaska, including the San Juan River in New Mexico; the Green River in Utah; the Wood in Idaho; and the Madison, Ruby, and Beaverhead in Montana. But, if the truth be known, central and southeast Oregon compares favorably with, and in many cases exceeds, the fly fishing I found in most other parts of the lower 48 states.

Fishing lakes and reservoirs is a whole different program than fishing streams. On streams, it's relatively easy to read the water and determine the feeding lanes and holds. That's not true with the still water of lakes. The surface is flat, without a lot of indicators to tell you where to fish. You have to look at the shoreline, identify submerged objects, study contour maps of the bottom, scan for surface activity, and observe where other people are fishing. You may need to keep moving and exploring until you find where the fish are active. This active spot can change from hour to hour.

To give you an example of what I'm talking about, I once had a banner day fishing Davis Lake. I fished the main lake, near the O'Dell Creek channel, with a small Adams pattern. Two days later I took my son Brad to this hot spot.

There were about eight other boats in the vicinity, which seemed to indicate that the fish were still working the area. We anchored and started fishing, while observing what kind of success other people were having. After about 45 minutes we hadn't had a rise and had seen only one other fish being taken. I switched to a nymph with the same results: nothing. About this time, we noted several fish working the reed beds on the edge of the channel. We pulled anchor and headed toward the rising fish. We positioned the boat, anchored, switched to dry patterns, and started casting toward the reeds. The first cast produced a rise but no fish. That was the last fish we'd see coming to a dry pattern. We didn't do any better with Montanas or Leeches either. We then moved well into the channel just before calling it a day.

On the way in, I put on a Prince nymph and cast toward the reeds. After several casts I hooked a nice fish. We anchored. Over the next hour we enjoyed catching and releasing a dozen rainbows ranging from 13 to 20 inches. This was just a case of observing, moving, changing patterns, and plain old fishermen's luck.

The message I convey is simple. *Don't get too enamored with what happened yesterday or that morning, rather, concentrate on finding where the fish are when you're on the water.* There are times when you'll need all your skill and luck to accomplish this. And here's a word of advice: Always get information.

No matter where you're going fly fishing, there is a right time to be there, a right technique, and a right fly pattern. Ask someone or check reputable literature (like this guide). Your best bet, in many cases, is to call a fly shop in the region. Several good ones are listed in the Resources section of this guide.

Permit me a word on words. Like the cover says, this is a "no nonsense" guide. I've tried to eliminate a lot of small talk, flowery adjectives, and unimportant folderol. This is an easy-to-read guide with essential and basic information. It will help you decide what water to visit and give you what you'll need to know to have a good time fly fishing.

When you're fishing central and southeast Oregon rivers, streams, lakes, and reservoirs (or any place, for that matter) please practice conservation. Catch and release is a good way to start, and consider these five guidelines that all conscientious fly fishers obey.

- Abide by the laws and fishing regulations.
- Respect property owners' rights.
- Be considerate of others.
- Never crowd in on another fisher.
- Carry out your litter.

Well-stocked fly boxes for fishing central Oregon's high lakes. Photo by Brian O'Keefe.

A Hosmer Lake brook trout. Photo by Dante Willerton.

Some Oregon Basics

In the central and southeast regions of Oregon, there are hundreds of lakes and reservoirs and miles and miles of rivers and creeks. I've not included all of these waters in this guide, but rather selected those that I've fished with success and that are readily accessible to the public. I've also included comments on eight private (fee-fishing) lakes, but only because Jeff and I feel they're worth the price of admission. Here are some basics you should scan and know before deciding what water to go fly fish.

Game Fish

Rainbow, brown, cutthroat, brook, steelhead, and bull trout are found throughout central Oregon. Other species include kokanee salmon, bass, and a variety of panfish.

Catch & Release

Many Oregon waters have limited-kill regulations. Responsible anglers practice catch and release and are careful handling fish.

Weather

High desert weather can be warm and ideal or very, very cold and windy. Weather in the Cascade Mountains can change quickly from comfortable to rainy, windy, or snowy. Be prepared for extreme weather in this region at any time of year. Always take, at least, a windbreaker or extra coat, hat, sunglasses, water, extra dry clothing, sunscreen, and a map.

Hazards & Safety

Use a wading staff in rivers like the Deschutes and other big streams that have fast currents and rocky bottoms. Don't drink the water unless you've purified it. Unfortunately, giardia is fairly common. Use caution with fires when camping. There are fire restrictions in many camping areas. Packing a cell phone is a good idea. Always tell someone where you are going and when you expect to return.

Rods

An all-around rod for this region is a 9-foot 5 weight. You can fish most waters in this guidebook with this size and weight. For small creeks try an 8-foot 3 weight rod. Float tubers prefer 9½ to 10-foot rods.

Reels

Palm, click, or disk drags work fine for most central Oregon fly waters. About 75 yards of backing is adequate for most species of trout. You'll need more for steelhead.

Lines & Leaders

You can use a floating line for almost all streams and still waters in our region. Occasionally, a sink tip or sinking line is an advantage. Some lakes and reservoirs fish better with a type-2 fast sinking and an intermediate sinking line. Leaders should be stout for sinking lines, 2X to 4X. For dry fly fishing and nymphing, 9- to 12-foot leaders, 4X to 6X, are about right.

Flies

The types of flies are listed here, but the sizes have been excluded. Depending on conditions, hatch sizes can vary greatly. Consult a local fly shop for the current sizes.

Wading Gear

I suggest using felt-soled wading boots, breathable waders, and a wading staff for almost every water in the region. A wading staff and cleats are helpful and recommended while fly fishing in the Deschutes. Wet-wading is possible during the summer months, especially in the eastern part of the state. Float tubers need breathable chest-high waders and warm clothes. Mountain waters are *cold*.

A healthy rainbow from the Middle Deschutes.
Photo by Eric Dunne.

A beautiful wild Metolius River rainbow trout.
Photo by John Judy.

Guides

If you are new to the sport, or to Oregon, a day outing with a qualified guide will help you learn the ropes. Check with the fly shops in the Resources section of this guidebook for waters that permit guided fly fishing.

Private Fly Fishing Waters

Paying for a day or two at a private water can be rewarding. If you are a fly fishing novice, private waters offer a great way to hone your skills. The private waters listed toward the back of this guidebook can offer excellent fishing in remote or isolated locations. They are a good value and are worth your consideration.

Trash

Leaving an area cleaner than you found it is the responsibility of all fly fishers.

Ratings

Each river, stream, lake, and reservoir in the main section of this guide has been rated on a scale from 1 to 10. A 10 water is one that offers the best possible fly fishing experience Oregon has to offer. A 1 would be fishable but not much else.

These ratings are based on my experiences of fly fishing these waters over a number of years. Thus, my rating may not necessarily coincide with the experience you have on your particular day of fly fishing, or even your combined experience. These ratings are best used to get a general idea of a particular fly fishing destination and as a means of comparing our opinions. But enough of the obvious stuff. Here's hoping you hook that fish you've always dreamed of on one of the waters in this guide.

Common Oregon Game Fish

Illustrations by Joseph R. Tomelleri.

Rainbow Trout

'Deschutes Redside' Rainbow Trout

Brown Trout

Bull Trout

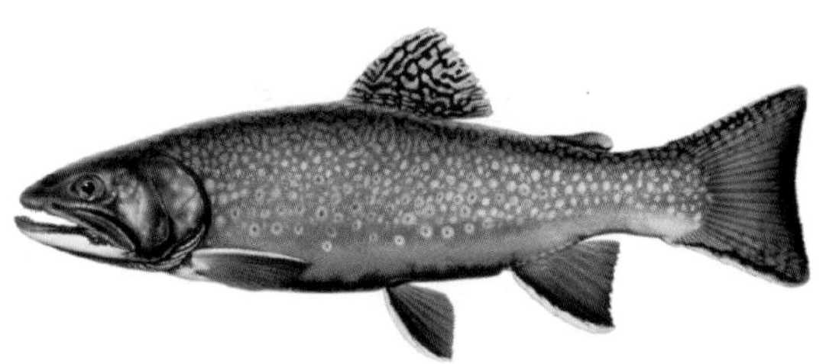

Brook Trout

Lahontan Cutthroat Trout

Lake Trout

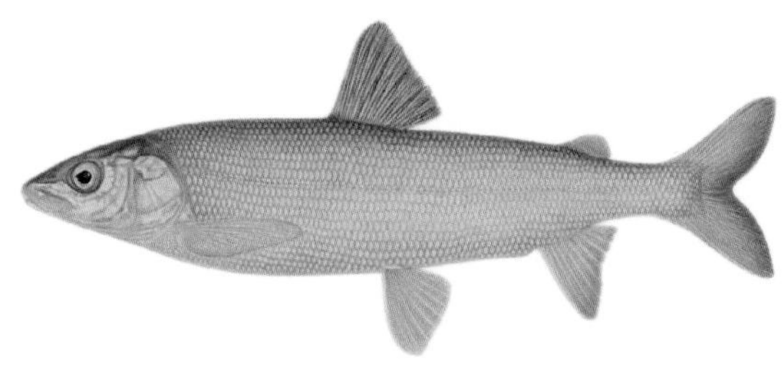

Mountain Whitefish

Steelhead Trout

Landlocked Atlantic Salmon

Largemouth Bass

Smallmouth Bass

Black Crappie

White Crappie

Kokanee Salmon (spawning male)

Chinook Salmon

Flies to Use in Oregon

Adams Parachute

Adams

Blue Winged Olive

Parachute Light Cahill

Comparadun

Pale Morning Dun

Elk Hair Caddis

Slow Water Caddis

X Caddis

Royal Wulff

Renegade

Stimulator

Sofa Pillow

Bullet Head Golden Stone

Humpy

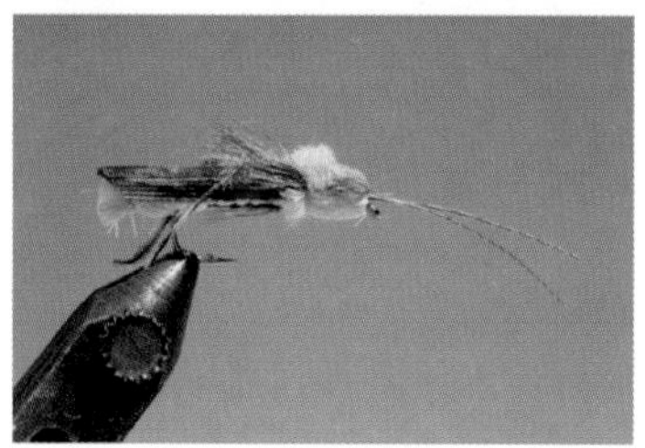
Whit's Hopper

Palomino Midge

Beadhead Prince Nymph

Beadhead Pheasant Tail — Beadhead Hare's Ear Nymph — Brassie

Kaufmann Stone — Girdle Bug — Marabou Damsel Nymph

Woolly Bugger — Krystal Bugger — Muddler Minnow

Max Canyon — Redwing Blackbird — Green Butt Skunk

Freight Train — Silver Hilton — Purple Peril

Zonker — Clouser Minnow Deep — Whitlock's Deer Hair Popper

Photos by Pete Chadwell.

Hatch Chart

No Hatch

Possible Hatch

Prime Hatch

	January	February	March	April	May	June	July	August	September	October	November	December
Caddisflies												
American Grannom (Brachycentrus) *Pupa and egg-laying adults most active.*												
Black Dancers (Mystacides) *Especially important around lake shores.*												
Brown Sedge (Lepidostoma) *Try brown Elk Hair Caddis for searching.*												
Green Sedge (Rhyacophila) *Larva commonly called Green Rockworm .*												
Little Sister Sedge (Cheumatopsyche) *Important caddis—wide distribution.*												
Little Western Dark Sedge *Important caddis; spent pattern is fun to fish!*												
Little Western Weedy Water Sedge *Dead drift small green pupa in riffles and weed beds.*												
Longhorned Sedge (Oecetis) *Great hatch on lakes, especially on edges.*												
Micro-caddis (various) *Size 18 to 24 in black or brown.*												
October Caddis (Dicosmoecus) *Pupa patterns usually best for bull trout, steelhead.*												
Pale Western Stream Sedge *Evening hatch; fish yellow pupa 20 behind adult.*												
Saddle Case Maker (Glossosoma) *Small cream larva is good in riffles, best in spring.*												
Silver Stripe Sedge (Hesperophylax) *Hatches odd times of year. Pupa usually best.*												
Spotted Sedge (Hydropsyche) *Important in mid- and large -sized streams.*												
Traveling Sedge (Limnephilidae) *Hatches on high lakes on warm evenings.*												
Tube Case Maker (Heliopsyche) *Good spring creek hatch, slower sections of rivers.*												
Damselflies *Nymphs most important; adults can cause chaos.*												
Dragonflies *Nymphs are most important.*												
Mayflies												
Blue Winged Olive (Baetis) *All Rivers; very prolific, important.*												
Cinygmula, Cinygma *Great early & late season hatch on Metolius.*												
Hexagenia *Important on Williamson River.*												

Hatch Chart

Key: No Hatch (white square) · Possible Hatch (light gray) · Prime Hatch (dark gray)

	January	February	March	April	May	June	July	August	September	October	November	December
Mayflies (continued)												
March Brown (Rithrogena) *Especially on Deschutes & McKenzie River.*			Prime	Prime	Prime							
Mahogany Dun (Paraleptophlebia) *Good hatches on Deschutes, Fall, Metolius, Crooked.*						Possible	Possible	Prime	Prime	Prime		
Pale Evening Dun (Heptogenia) *Strong hatches on Deschutes.*				Possible	Prime	Prime	Prime	Prime	Prime	Possible		
Pale Morning Dun (Ephemerella) *Important on all rivers and spring creeks.*				Possible	Prime	Prime	Prime	Prime	Prime	Possible		
Speckle-wing Dun (Callibaetis) *Super stillwater hatch.*				Possible	Prime	Prime	Prime	Prime	Prime	Possible		
Trico (Tricorythodes) *Good hatches on Ana River & Williamson River.*						Possible	Prime	Prime	Prime	Possible		
Western Green Drake (Drunella) *Fall, McKenzie, Deschutes and especially Metolius.*					Possible	Prime	Prime		Prime	Prime		
Midges (Chironomidae) *Very important on all rivers and lakes.*	Possible	Prime	Prime	Prime	Prime	Possible	Possible	Possible	Prime	Prime	Prime	Possible
Scud *Fish them in lakes and rivers.*	Possible	Prime	Prime	Prime	Possible	Possible	Possible	Possible	Prime	Prime	Prime	Possible
Stoneflies												
Little Black Stone *Early season if water conditions are right.*	Possible	Prime	Prime									
Little Olive Stone *Late afternoon and evenings, especially on Metolius.*								Prime	Prime	Prime		
Golden Stone (Hesperoperla pacifica) *Lower Deschutes River.*					Prime	Prime	Possible					
Golden Stone (Hesperoperla pacifica) *Metolius River.*							Prime	Prime	Possible	Possible		
Salmon Fly (Pteronarcys californica) *Lower Deschutes River.*					Prime	Prime						
Salmon Fly (Pteronarcys californica) *Metolius River.*							Prime	Prime	Prime	Possible		
Yellow Sally *Cold rivers on warm days for this hatch.*							Prime	Prime	Prime			
Terrestrials *Ants and hoppers productive, also beetle patterns.*					Possible	Possible	Possible	Prime	Prime	Prime		
Waterboatman *Mostly in lakes.*				Possible	Prime	Prime	Prime					

Fly Fishing Conditions by the Month

Here are general fly fishing conditions for central and southeastern Oregon. Use this table to help plan your fly fishing outing or vacation. Water conditions can vary from year to year, as can seasons and regulations, affecting the information I give here. Always consult a fly shop to get the latest information.

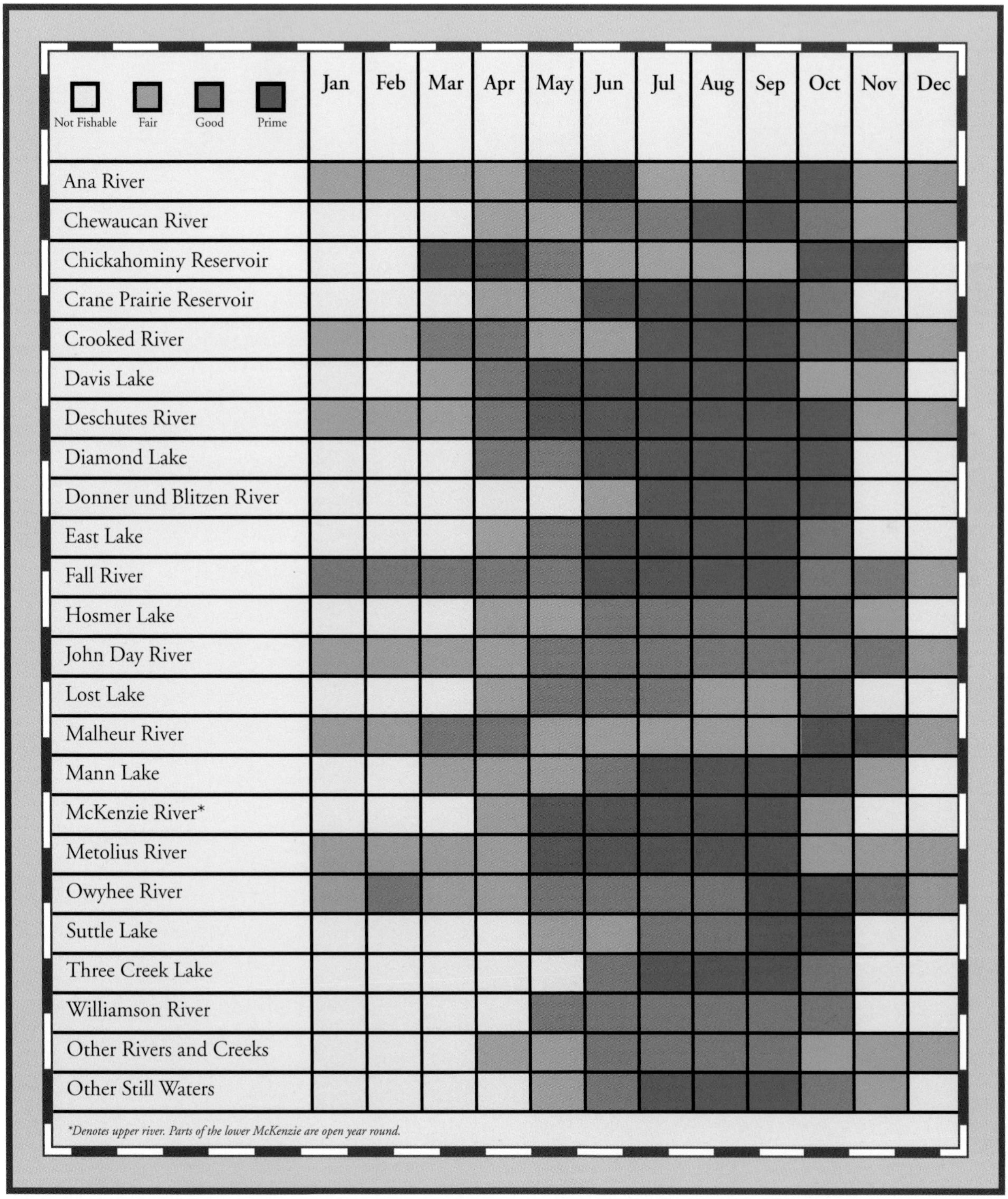

Not Fishable / Fair / Good / Prime	Jan	Feb	Mar	Apr	May	Jun	Jul	Aug	Sep	Oct	Nov	Dec
Ana River												
Chewaucan River												
Chickahominy Reservoir												
Crane Prairie Reservoir												
Crooked River												
Davis Lake												
Deschutes River												
Diamond Lake												
Donner und Blitzen River												
East Lake												
Fall River												
Hosmer Lake												
John Day River												
Lost Lake												
Malheur River												
Mann Lake												
McKenzie River*												
Metolius River												
Owyhee River												
Suttle Lake												
Three Creek Lake												
Williamson River												
Other Rivers and Creeks												
Other Still Waters												

**Denotes upper river. Parts of the lower McKenzie are open year round.*

The rugged Crooked River canyon south of Prineville, Oregon. Photo by John Judy.

Top Oregon Fly Fishing Waters

Central & Southeastern

Photo by Aprille Chadwell.

Photo by Eric Dunne.

Photo by Pete Chadwell.

Photo by Pete Chadwell.

Photo by Fred Boos.

A lone angler searches for steelhead on the Lower Deschutes River. Photo by John Judy.

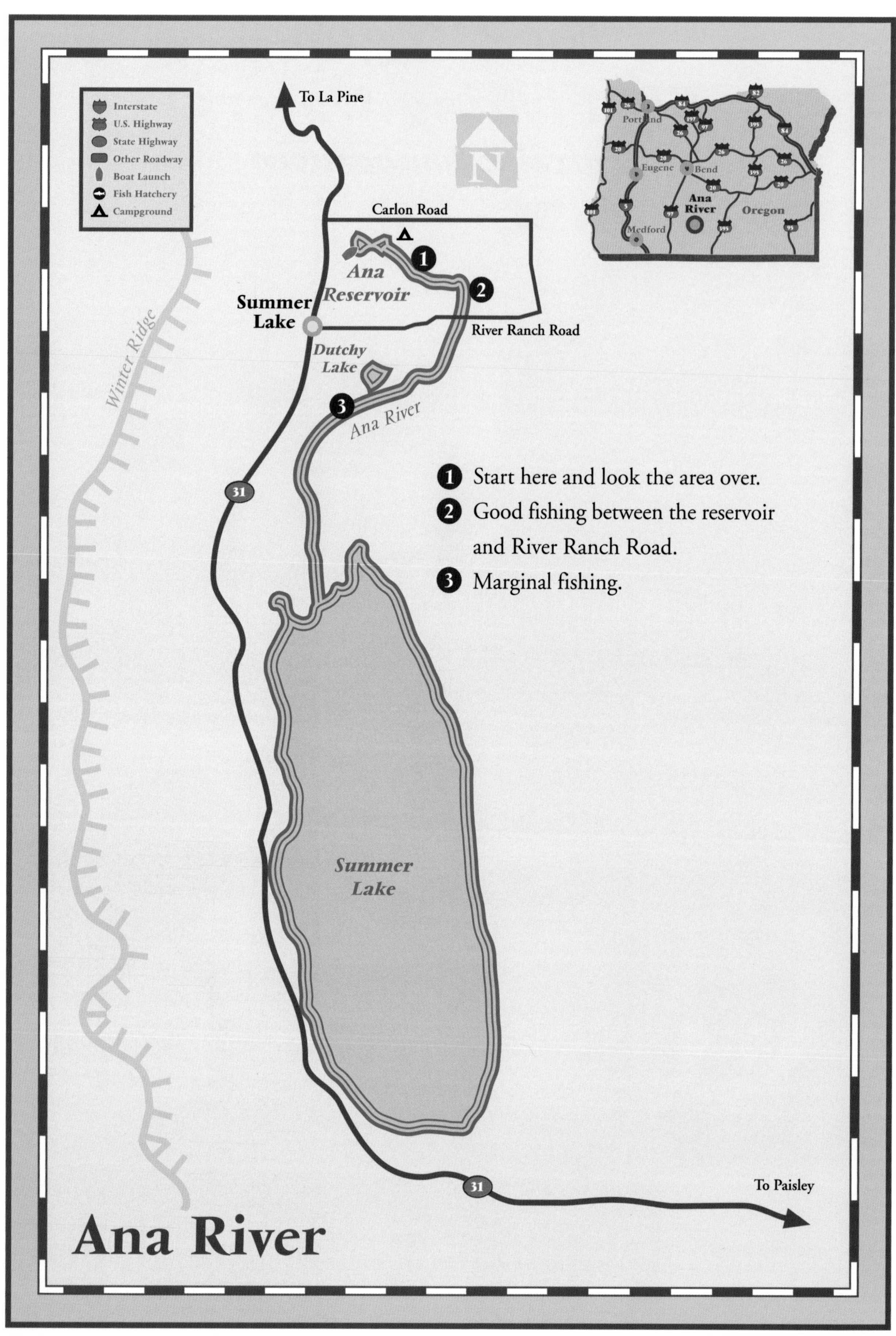
Interstate
U.S. Highway
State Highway
Other Roadway
Boat Launch
Fish Hatchery
Campground
To La Pine
N
Carlon Road
Ana
Reservoir
Summer
Lake
River Ranch Road
Dutchy
Lake
Ana River
Winter Ridge
31
Summer
Lake
31
To Paisley
Portland
Eugene
Bend
Medford
Ana
River
Oregon
1 Start here and look the area over.
2 Good fishing between the reservoir and River Ranch Road.
3 Marginal fishing.
Ana River

Ana River

The Ana River offers a unique fly fishing experience in an honest-to-God desert river. It flows through a sand-and-sagebrush open landscape that is genuine Oregon high desert. The river flows from Ana Reservoir and discharges into Summer Lake. The river's true origins are springs that are now covered by the Ana Reservoir.

The Ana is only about seven miles long, doesn't get much pressure, and holds some nice-sized rainbow trout, being stocked with 20,000 fingerling trout each year. The reservoir is stocked annually with catchable trout and every other year with bass fingerlings.

If you like fly fishing challenges, you'll like the Ana's clear water and the need to make good fly presentations. You'll work for what you get, and at times fishing can be frustrating because you can't get a fish to rise. I suggest you take the time to walk a quarter mile or so along the banks and determine if you want to wade. Look for insects while you are walking. You'll find an abundance of midges, mayflies, and terrestrials around the river.

The Ana River lies east of Highway 31 in the Great Basin near Summer Lake. If you are visiting central Oregon, the Ana is about a two-hour drive from Bend and is a good alternative to some of the area's more crowded waters.

An angler stalks trout on the Ana River. Photo by Brian O'Keefe.

Types of Fish
Mostly rainbow trout. These fish run from 8 to 16 inches and are great fighters.

Known Hatches
Midges, mayflies and terrestrials.

Equipment to Use
Rods: 2–5 weight, 7–9 feet in length.
Reels: Palm drag.
Lines: Floating, to match rod weight.
Leaders: 5X to 6X, 9–12 feet in length.
Wading: Use breathable waders with boots. A wading staff is a good idea. You can fish much of this river without wading.

Flies to Use
Dries: Adams, Pale Morning Dun, Renegade, Spinner, Callibaetis, Comparadun, Blue-Winged Olive, Trico, X Caddis, Henryville Special, CDC Caddis, Slow Water Caddis.
Nymphs: Hare's Ear, Chironomid Pupa, Zug Bug, Scud, Brassie, Serendipity, and Pheasant Tail.
Streamers: Leech, Woolly Bugger.

When to Fish
It's best to fish in May and June and September and October. The Ana River fishes best in the early morning and late evening.

Seasons & Limits
Generally this river is open year-round. Because regulations are subject to change, consult the Oregon Department of Fish & Wildlife regulations or a local fly shop before fishing.

Nearby Fly Fishing
In a weekend's time it is possible to fish the Ana River, Ana Reservoir, Lake of the Dunes, and the Chewaucan River (all of which are described in this guide).

Accommodations & Services
There is a store, restaurant, motel, and gas at Summer Lake. There are camping facilities near the dam at Ana Reservoir.

Rating
Harry's Opinion: If you happen to hit a good day, you'll come back for more of the Ana. A soft 4.

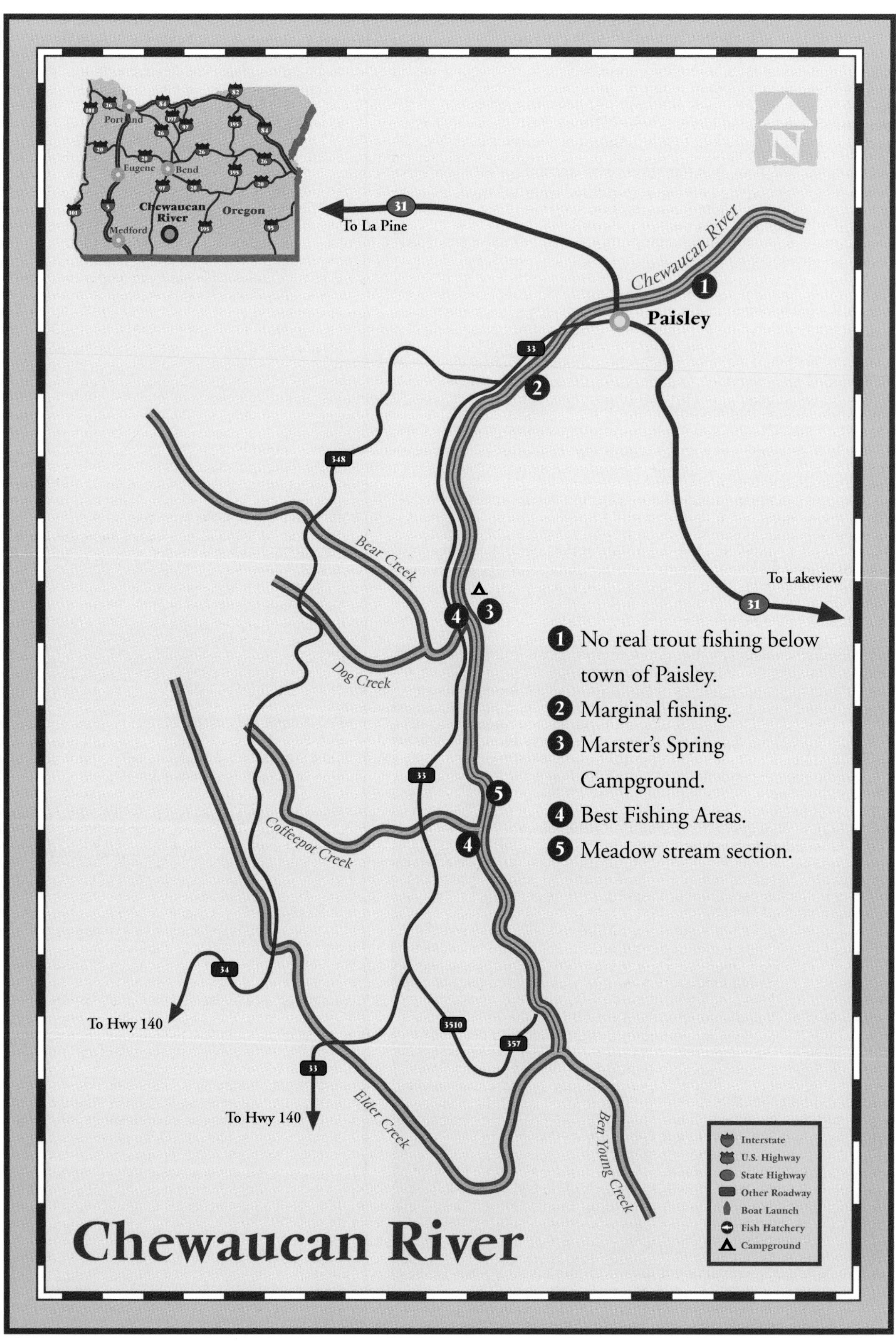
Portland
Eugene
Bend
Chewaucan River
Oregon
Medford
N
To La Pine
Chewaucan River
Paisley
To Lakeview
Bear Creek
Dog Creek
Coffeepot Creek
Elder Creek
Ben Young Creek
To Hwy 140
To Hwy 140
1 No real trout fishing below town of Paisley.
2 Marginal fishing.
3 Marster's Spring Campground.
4 Best Fishing Areas.
5 Meadow stream section.
Interstate
U.S. Highway
State Highway
Other Roadway
Boat Launch
Fish Hatchery
Campground
Chewaucan River

Chewaucan River

The Chewaucan is not a big river, but it is enjoyable to fish with a fly rod. It's a pretty river, off the beaten path, and not very crowded. If you are in the area fishing the Ana or Lake of the Dunes and want a more forested setting or a change of location, give the Chewaucan a try.

The Chewaucan flows out of the mountains and heads for the Great Basin, where it dissipates into the Oregon desert. As you go upstream from Paisley, you enter the Fremont National Forest. Much of the fishable river lies in this pine-studded drainage. The numbers of redband trout have gone down due to recent low-water conditions, but the fly fishing is still pretty good. Don't forget mosquito repellent. You'll need it!

To get to the Chewaucan, drive to the small town of Paisley near Summer Lake, on Highway 31. You'll need to turn to the south just west of Paisley to access the best part of the river. Paisley is a good rest stop when traveling through this rural area.

The Chewaucan River provides an uncrowded alternative. Photo by Matt Johnson.

Types of Fish

Predominantly planted rainbow trout from 8 to 12 inches. Some nice fish in the 14- to 16-inch range are taken on a regular basis.

Known Hatches

Mayflies, midges, and caddis.

Equipment to Use

Rods: 3–5 weight, 7–9 feet in length.
Reels: Palm drag.
Lines: Match floating and sink tip to rod weight.
Leaders: 4X and 5X, 9 feet in length.
Wading: Felt-soled hip boots are OK, but you're better off with lightweight waders with felt-soled wading shoes.

Flies to Use

Dries: Pale Morning Dun, Adams, Renegade, Royal Wulff, Mosquito, Comparadun, Elk Hair Caddis, H&L Variant, X Caddis, Humpy, CDC Caddis and Madam X, Blue-Winged Olive.
Nymphs: Pheasant Tail, Hare's Ear, Zug Bug, Caddis Pupa, Beadhead Soft Hackle PT, Beadhead Flashback Hare's Ear and Beadhead Prince.

When to Fish

Regulars on the Chewaucan seem to prefer July through October. Late afternoon and evening are generally the best times to fish.

Seasons & Limits

The Chewaucan usually opens in late April and closes in late October, although these dates can change. Check with a fly shop or consult the Oregon Department of Fish & Wildlife regulations for exact dates and limits.

Nearby Fly Fishing

Ana River, Lake of the Dunes.

Accommodations & Services

The town of Paisley has a service station, diner, and motel, as does Summer Lake, which also has a B&B and a nearby hot spring spa. There is camping at selected spots along the river.

Rating

Harry's Opinion: I like the Chewaucan. Even though it's not a highly rated stream, I feel it's worth the trip. Exploring new territory is part of the fun of fly fishing. Normally, the Chewaucan is a 4, but if you hit "one of those days," it can be an 8 or 9.

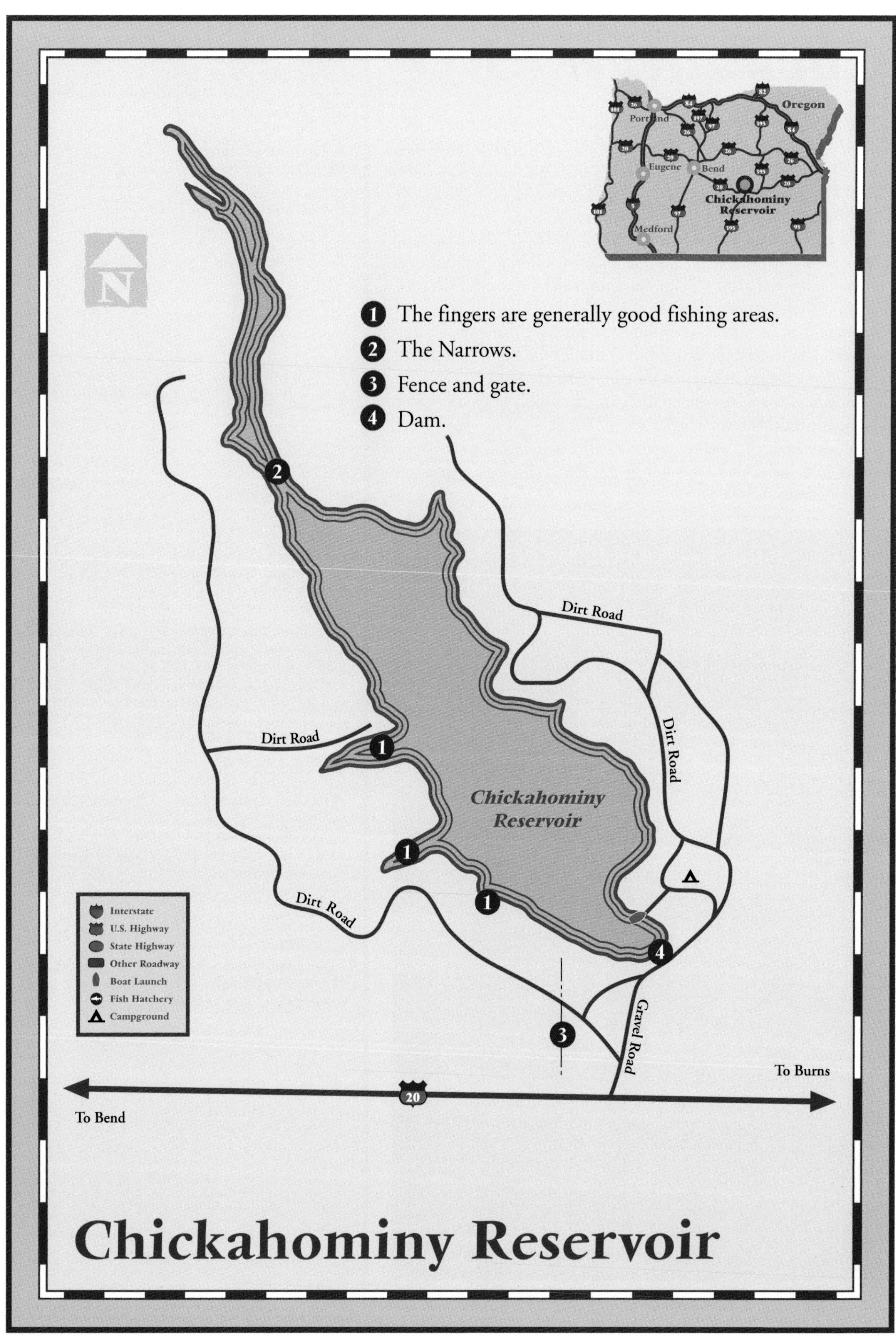

Oregon
Portland
Eugene
Bend
Medford
Chickahominy Reservoir
N
1 The fingers are generally good fishing areas.
2 The Narrows.
3 Fence and gate.
4 Dam.
Dirt Road
Dirt Road
Dirt Road
Dirt Road
Chickahominy Reservoir
Gravel Road
Interstate
U.S. Highway
State Highway
Other Roadway
Boat Launch
Fish Hatchery
Campground
To Burns
To Bend
20
Chickahominy Reservoir

Chickahominy Reservoir

As of the summer 2003, the water conditions at Chickahominy were unfavorable: This once-great fly fishing reservoir was closed after years of little precipitation and low water levels. and many fish died. Check with the Oregon Department of Fish & Wildlife or a local fly shop before going to "Chick." Take note, however, of what *can* happen, and maybe the place will be back on your list by the time you read this.

When Chickahominy is at full pool, it can grow big fish and grow them fast. The 100,000 rainbows planted here annually can grow to better than 20 inches. Indications are they grow up to two inches a month during the summer season.

The reservoir is in dry, treeless, high desert country, about 100 miles east of Bend, the hub of central Oregon. It's a favorite of Bend-area anglers and others traveling the east-west route from Idaho or Burns to central Oregon (Highway 20, the Central Oregon Highway). The area was developed by the Oregon Department of Fish & Wildlife as an angler's reservoir and is a good-sized body of water covering roughly 500 acres.

Fly fish the reservoir as you would most others. The best results have been with wet patterns or streamers. Fish them near the rocky shore and weed beds. Let the fly sink and strip it in with irregular tugs of four to six inches of line. Float tubers should do the same, or let a Prince, Woolly Bugger, Boatman, Leech or Damsel-type pattern sink very deep and retrieve it slowly. Sink tip lines help with this technique.

There are campgrounds, drinking water, and restrooms at the reservoir, along with a boat ramp. Weather in the spring and fall can be unpredictable, so be prepared for wind and cold. The summer months are generally hot, and fly fishing is poor, unless perhaps there is a hatch here and there or if you fish the deep water near the dam. A word of caution: Do not drive on the dirt roads around the reservoir after a rainstorm, as they get very muddy.

Sunset over Chickahominy Reservoir.
Photo by Brian O'Keefe.

Types of Fish
Rainbow trout. The fish are stocked annually as three-inch fingerlings and grow rapidly.

Known Hatches
Damselflies, midges, and mayflies.

Equipment to Use
Rods: 5–7 weight, 8½–9 feet in length.
Reels: Palm or mechanical drag.
Lines: Floating, sink tip, or intermediate.
Leaders: 4X to 5X, 7–12 feet in length.
Wading: Chest-high neoprene or breathable waders with felt-soled wading shoes. A float tube or pontoon-type boat is a good way to fish the reservoir.

Flies to Use
My best results have been with wet patterns: Prince, Hare's Ear, Zug Bug, Damsel, Woolly Bugger, Carey Special.

When to Fish
You'll find the best fly fishing about a week after the ice melts off, which is about March 15. You'll have good fishing for about a month. Fishing can be slow in the summer, but it picks up again in late September until the reservoir freezes.

Seasons & Limits
Once the reservoir reopens, it is open year around. Limits can vary, so check with a fly shop or consult the Oregon Department of Fish & Wildlife regulations for current information.

Accommodations & Services
There is camping at the reservoir but nothing else. Bring whatever you need with you because it's a 40-mile drive to Burns, the nearest town. There is a store and service station at Riley, seven miles away, but the hours of operation can be inconsistent.

Rating
Harry's Opinion: Chickahominy does not get a lot of pressure, and the fishing can be outstanding. Just be prepared for the weather. Spring and fall, it's a 7.5. During the summer, it's a 2.

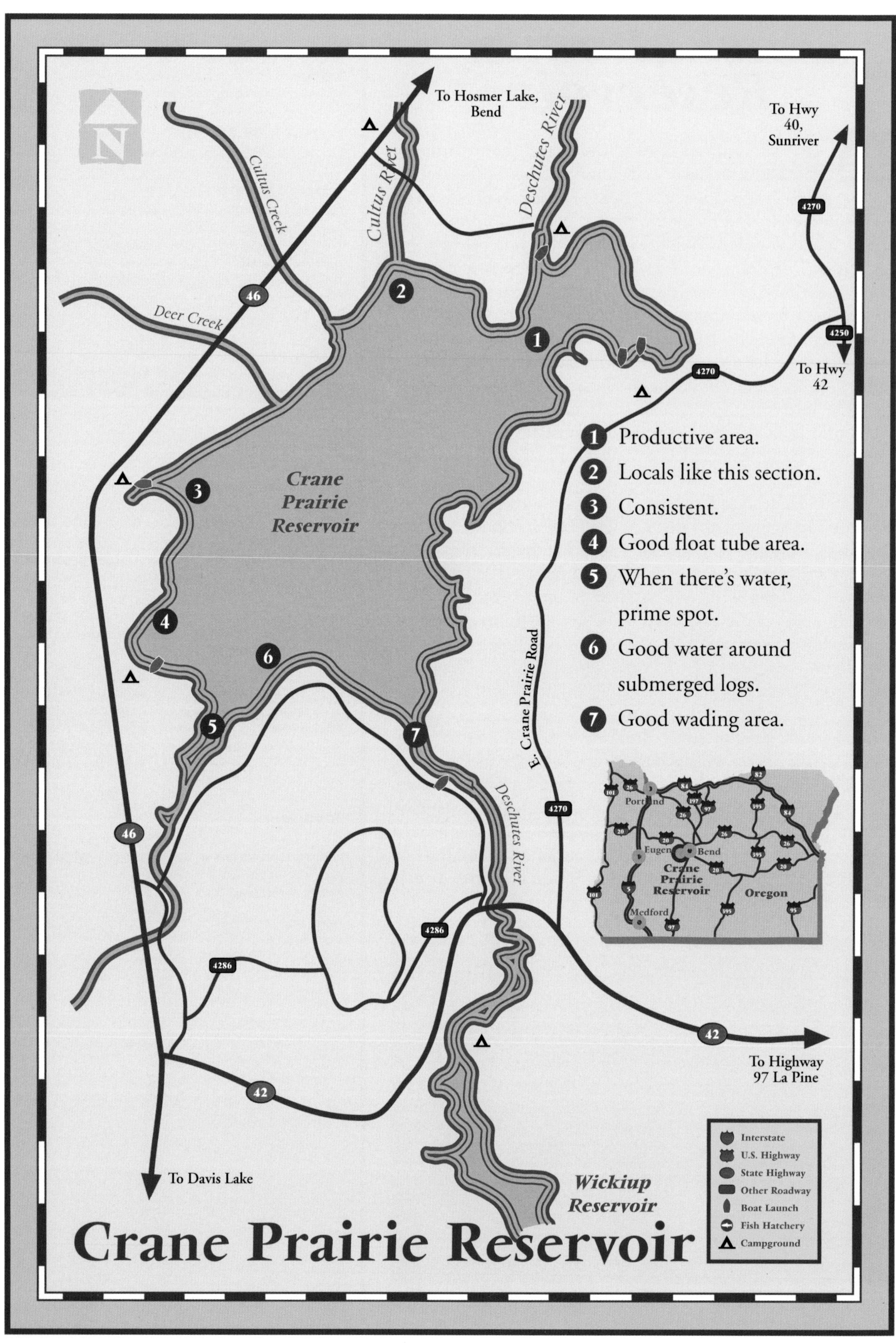

Crane Prairie Reservoir

Crane Prairie Reservoir

Crane Prairie is one of the finest fly fishing reservoirs in the West. It has more than its share of big trout, scenery, and wildlife viewing opportunities. The famed Deschutes River fills this reservoir and, though the lake is not very deep (11 to 20 feet), water levels are fairly consistent. Fish enjoy good cover and plenty of insects.

Most people fish the reservoir from a boat or float tube. Try trolling large streamers and other wet flies. Nymphing works well early in the season. Fish near Crane's distinctive submerged trees and stick-ups and close to the shoreline when the water is high. In low-water conditions look for the two main (submerged) river channels.

Crane Prairie lies west of Bend, Oregon, and can be accessed from Century Drive. This is the road past the Mt. Bachelor Ski Area and other Cascade lakes. Also look for Highway 46 or Highway 40 from Sunriver.

This is *big* trout water, so you'll need equipment that can handle large fish. Bring your larger, heavier-weight rods. You'll be glad you did if it's windy or you get into one of the big fish here. Hatchery fish are marked with an adipose fin clip or left ventral clip. In the late 1990s, panfish (bluegill and crappie) became a problem. As of this writing, removing these fish is permitted.

The submerged trees at Crane Prairie provide cover for big rainbows. Photo by Brian O'Keefe.

Types of Fish

You'll find rainbow and brook trout with a fair population of kokanee and illegally introduced bass. The size of these trout is amazing: three- to five- pound fish are common, and fish in the 10-pound range are recorded annually.

Known Hatches

Crane has a real smorgasbord of aquatic food for the trout. Damselflies, dragonflies, mayflies, scuds, and leeches make up a portion of the buffet.

Equipment to Use

Rods: 6 and 7 weight, 9–10 feet in length.
Reels: Mechanical and palm drag.
Lines: Matching floating, sink tip, or slow sinking lines.
Leaders: 3X to 5X, 9–12 feet in length, fluorocarbon is best.
Wading: For the most part, fishing from a floating device is most productive. There are a few places where wading can be very rewarding. Try the arm near the dam. Chest-high waders and wading boots are desirable.

Flies to Use

Dries: Parachute Callibaetis, Two-Feather Mayfly, Captive Dun, Callibaetis Spinner, Timberline Emerger, Comparadun, Adams, Goddard Caddis, Adult Damsel, Slow Water Caddis, Black Elk Hair Caddis, Griffith's Gnat, Palomino, Century Drive Midge, Light Cahill in smaller sizes.
Nymphs & Streamers: Prince, Scud, Hare's Ear, Pheasant Tail, Snail, Callibaetis, Chironomid, Montana, Woolly Bugger, Leech, Damsel, Dragon, San Juan Worm.

When to Fish

June through September are the best months to fish Crane Prairie Reservoir, but good fishing can also be experienced in April, May and October.

Seasons & Limits

The season opens in late April and closes at the end of October. For exact dates and limit regulations, refer to the Oregon Department of Fish & Wildlife regulations.

Accommodations & Services

Crane Prairie is blessed with good camping facilities. A store, food service, and gas are available at the resort at Gales Landing. In the vicinity is Twin Lakes Resort, and complete services are available at Sunriver, La Pine, and Bend.

Rating

Harry's Opinion: If you have time to fish only one place on your trip to central Oregon and want the opportunity to catch trophy fish, test your skills at Crane Prairie Reservoir. An 8.5.

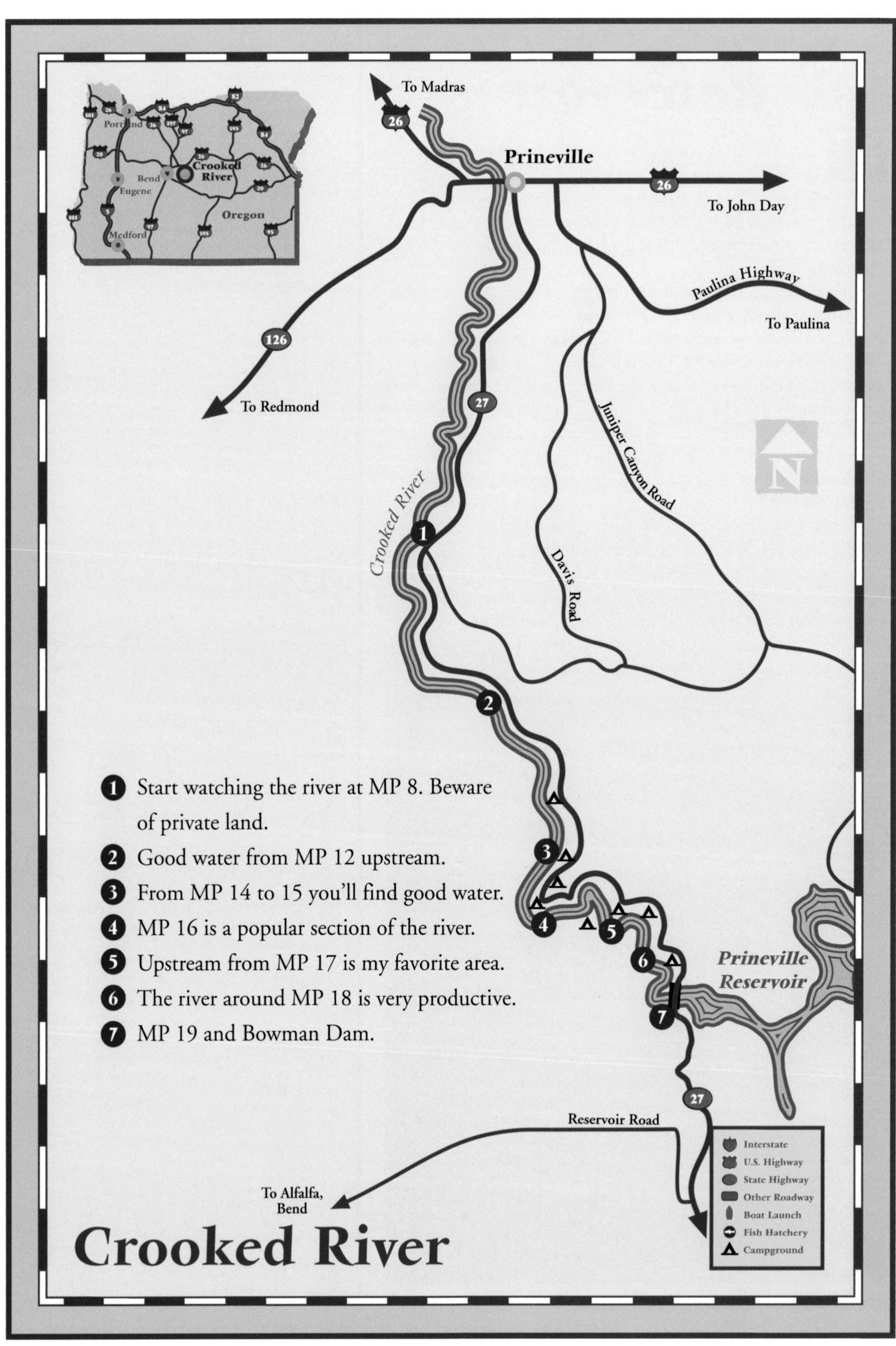

1. Start watching the river at MP 8. Beware of private land.
2. Good water from MP 12 upstream.
3. From MP 14 to 15 you'll find good water.
4. MP 16 is a popular section of the river.
5. Upstream from MP 17 is my favorite area.
6. The river around MP 18 is very productive.
7. MP 19 and Bowman Dam.

Crooked River

Crooked River

This is the river most central Oregon fly fishers head to when winter weather is bad and fishing is off in other places. The primary fishing section of the Crooked is often under clear and dry midwinter skies and the only game in town. This section lies just south of the town of Prineville.

The 19 miles from Prineville to Bowman Dam is reached off paved State Highway 27 which parallels the river. The Crooked River below Bowman Dam is a wonderful tailrace stream. That is, it's wonderful when the Bureau of Reclamation releases an adequate amount of water (minimum of 74 cubic feet per second) to sustain quality fishing. From Mileposts 12 to 19, which is really the prime area, you'll find interesting water with plenty of riffles and pools.

The area's topographical features are impressive. High basalt walls and juniper, pine, and sage-covered flats create an environment right out of a Wild West movie set. Most of the time the water is off-color, but don't let that bother you—it doesn't seem to bother the fish.

The Crooked is primarily a nymphing stream. Use a strike indicator when fishing these patterns. Dry fly activity can be good, but you have to be there when the hatch is on. Day in and day out, most fish are taken subsurface.

The Crooked River winds through a beautiful desert canyon. Photo by Pete Chadwell.

Types of Fish

Rainbows, cutthroats, and a rainbow-cutthroat cross. Most fish will run from 8 to 12 inches, but you'll get a fair number in the 13- to 18-inch range. Jeff and I have seen pictures of fish bigger than six pounds, but I haven't hooked one.

Known Hatches

The basic food of the fish here is a scud, often called a freshwater shrimp. They're in the river by the zillions.

Equipment to Use

Rods: 1–5 weight, 6–9 feet in length.
Reels: Palm drag.
Lines: Match line to rod weight. Floating lines with weighted nymphs produce.
Leaders: 5X and 6X, 9 feet in length.
Wading: The Crooked is not necessarily difficult to wade if you use good judgment, but it's tricky. There are lots of boulders that can cause embarrassing problems—not life threatening but they can make you look like an unskilled gymnast. I suggest felt-soled wading boots, a wading staff, and at least waist-high breathable waders.

Flies to Use

Dries: Adams, Comparadun, Elk Hair Caddis, Renegade, Griffith's Gnat, Midge Pupa, Palomino, Blue-Winged Olive, Knock Down Dun, Hi-Viz Parachute, Micro Mayfly.
Nymphs & Streamers: Scud, Brassie, Beadhead Prince, Hare's Ear, Pheasant Tail, Serendipity Beadhead, Soft Hackle, Woolly Bugger.

When to Fish

Open year-round, so you should fish here whenever you've got the time. Occasionally in the winter months the Crooked freezes over, so check first. In my opinion, the Crooked fishes well all day long, with the best time being in the late afternoon and evening.

Seasons & Limits

The Crooked is open year-round, but restrictions on fish limits and fishing methods are subject to change. Refer to the Oregon Department of Fish & Wildlife regulations for current information.

Accommodations & Services

There are fine camping areas, provided by the Bureau of Land Management, all along the river. Lodging can be found 25 miles away in Prineville. There's a full range of services available there, including restaurants, groceries, lodging, gas, and automotive services.

Rating

Harry's Opinion: I like the Crooked from Mileposts 12 to 19. There are plenty of fish, and it's a good stream for all skill levels. A 6.5.

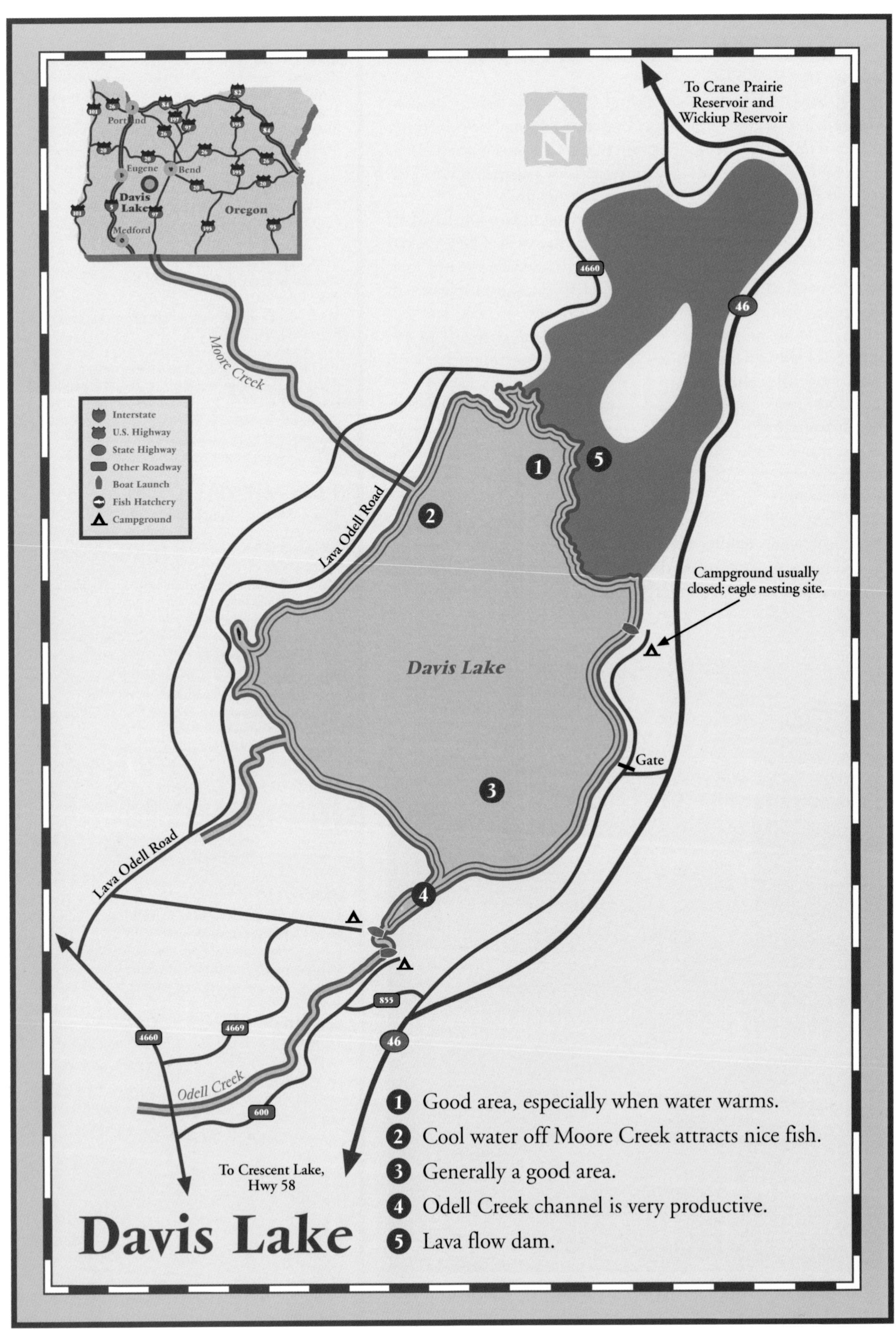

To Crane Prairie Reservoir and Wickiup Reservoir
Portland
Eugene
Bend
Davis Lake
Oregon
Medford
Moore Creek
Interstate
U.S. Highway
State Highway
Other Roadway
Boat Launch
Fish Hatchery
Campground
4660
46
Lava Odell Road
Davis Lake
Campground usually closed; eagle nesting site.
Gate
Lava Odell Road
855
4669
4660
46
Odell Creek
600
To Crescent Lake, Hwy 58
Davis Lake
1 Good area, especially when water warms.
2 Cool water off Moore Creek attracts nice fish.
3 Generally a good area.
4 Odell Creek channel is very productive.
5 Lava flow dam.

Davis Lake

Davis Lake is another water that has been lower than normal recently, reducing the numbers of fish. When Davis is right, it's one fine and challenging, fly fishing only fishery. It's only about 25 feet deep and is thick with bugs. Catch and release fishing has taught the large trout to remain even more skeptical than usual. Nymphing is generally the best technique on Davis, but dries can be productive.

Davis Lake is located in both Deschutes and Klamath counties. It's about nine miles past Crane Prairie and Wickiup reservoirs and the Twin Lakes. If any of these other waters is off, go a little farther south to Davis. Davis, managed for fly angling, has generally lived up to its goal of providing big trout. During the central Oregon drought of the late 1980s, as in the 2000–2003 period, the lake suffered from low water conditions and relatively poor fishing was the norm. Disease also reduced the number and hardiness of Davis trout. Water levels are improving, and the lake will return to its glory days.

Fishing while using a motor used to be prohibited, though as of now one can use a motor while fishing and to get to the fishing spot. Check to make sure this is the current rule at Davis. A motor is a benefit on a lake some three miles across. Use a float tube just about anywhere on the lake during cool-water months. During summer, most of the fish head toward the inlets and the lava dam area. Bald eagles nest near the Lava Flow Campground area, so camping is usually prohibited except from September through December.

You can reach Davis Lake from the city of Bend by traveling South on U.S. Highway 97 and turning right onto Vandevert Road. At the intersection of Vandevert Road and South Century Drive, turn left, then turn right again at South Century Drive, which is also County Route 42. Continue on 42 until it intersects with County Route 46 and turn left. Continue on 42 for approximately 9 miles and look for the main access road to Davis Lake on the West side of County Route 46.

Fishing the weed beds at Davis Lake.
Photo by Brian O'Keefe.

Types of Fish

Primarily rainbow trout; other species have been introduced by the Oregon Department of Fish & Wildlife but are no longer found. Largemouth bass have been taking hold since their illegal introduction in 1995. When Davis is at its best, two- to five- pound trout are common.

Known Hatches

Davis is rich with aquatic life. There are midges, mayfly, and mosquito hatches.

Equipment to Use

Rods: 5–7 weight, 8½–9½ feet in length.
Reels: Mechanical and palm drag.
Lines: Floating and sink tip to match rod weight.
Leaders: 4X and 5X, 9 feet in length.
Wading: You can wade some portions of the lake. You should have chest-high neoprenes with wading boots. Davis is a good float tubing lake, especially around the O'Dell Creek channel. Boats (type and design of your choice) are in order. There are launching sites at all the campgrounds.

Flies to Use

Dries: Parachute Callibaetis, Two-Feather Mayfly, Captive Dun, Callibaetis Spinner, Timberline Emerger, Comparadun, Adams, Goddard Caddis, Adult Damsel, Slow Water Caddis, Black Elk Hair Caddis, Griffith's Gnat, Palomino, Century Drive Midge, Light Cahill in smaller sizes.
Nymphs & Streamers: Prince, Scud, Montana, Pheasant Tail, Snail, Callibaetis Nymph, Woolly Bugger, Boatman, Leech, Damsel, Hare's Ear Chironomid, San Juan Worm, Dragonfly.

When to Fish

When the water is right, good fishing is possible throughout the season. I feel the best time is late May or June and again in late September and October. My experience is that Davis fishes well all day long.

Seasons & Limits

Open all year but, before fishing, review the Oregon Department of Fish & Wildlife regulations for exact dates and limits.

Nearby Fly Fishing

Crane Prairie and Wickiup reservoirs, Twin Lakes.

Accommodations & Services

There are excellent campgrounds at Davis, but for most other services you'll have to drive to La Pine, Sunriver, or Bend. The resorts at South Twin Lake and Crane Prairie Reservoir have restaurants, groceries, and gas and may be open depending on the season.

Rating

Harry's Opinion: Davis has an abundance of food that grows big fish. Due to the recent introduction of a different strain of rainbow trout, Davis is one of the prime fly fishing lakes in Oregon. It is a solid 7.

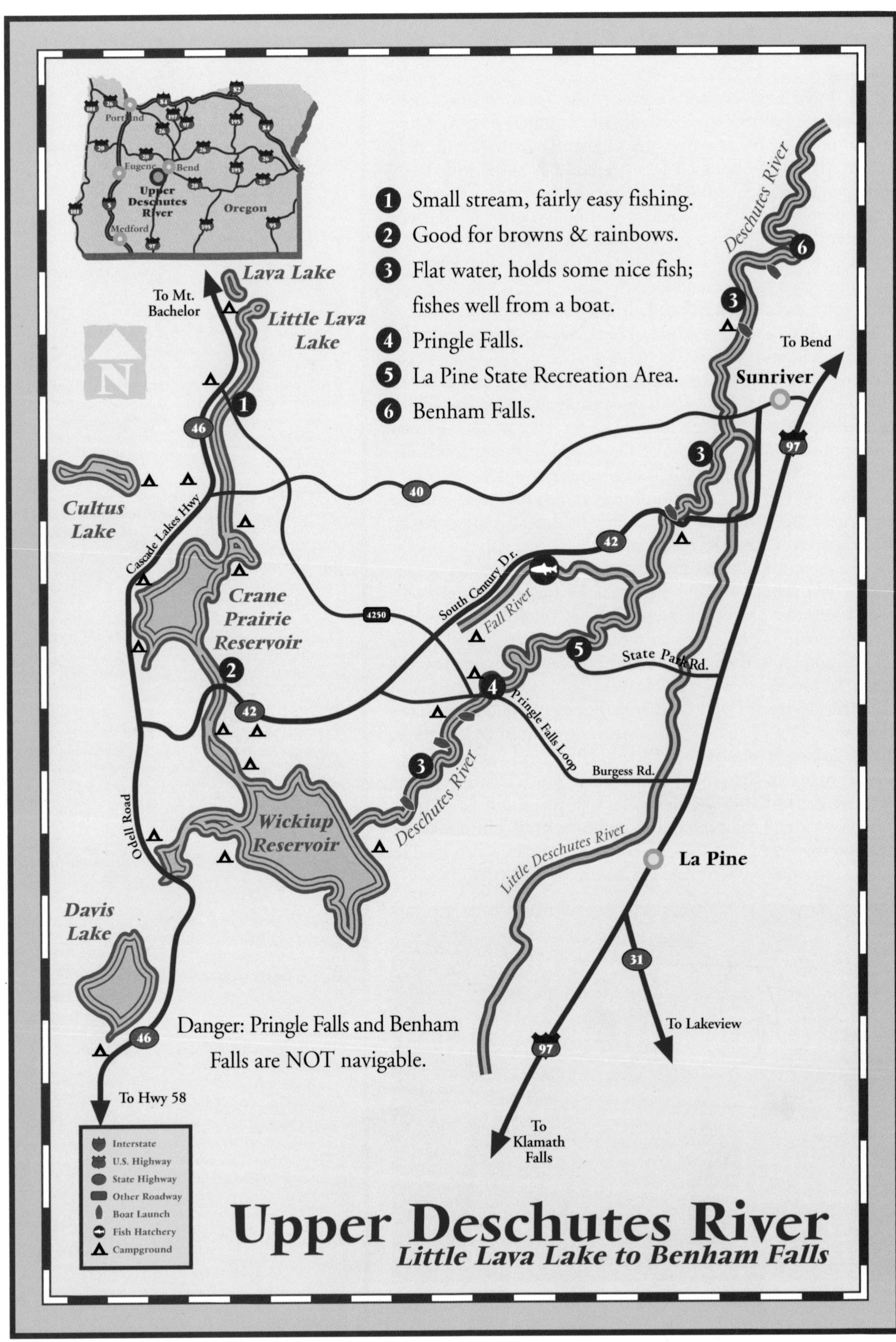
Upper Deschutes River
Little Lava Lake to Benham Falls
1 Small stream, fairly easy fishing.
2 Good for browns & rainbows.
3 Flat water, holds some nice fish; fishes well from a boat.
4 Pringle Falls.
5 La Pine State Recreation Area.
6 Benham Falls.
Danger: Pringle Falls and Benham Falls are NOT navigable.
Lava Lake
Little Lava Lake
To Mt. Bachelor
Cultus Lake
Cascade Lakes Hwy
Crane Prairie Reservoir
Wickiup Reservoir
Davis Lake
Odell Road
To Hwy 58
Deschutes River
Fall River
South Century Dr.
State Park Rd.
Pringle Falls Loop
Burgess Rd.
Little Deschutes River
Sunriver
To Bend
La Pine
To Lakeview
To Klamath Falls
Portland
Eugene
Bend
Medford
Oregon
Upper Deschutes River
Interstate
U.S. Highway
State Highway
Other Roadway
Boat Launch
Fish Hatchery
Campground

Deschutes River

If I could choose only one river to fish, the Deschutes would be it. It has it all: beauty, variety of fish, challenging water, and a true test of fly fishing skills. Yet it's possible to take a real neophyte to the river and, with some assistance, get him or her into fish.

For these and other reasons, the Deschutes is probably the finest overall fly fishing river in western America. Its complement of big redside trout, salmon, steelhead, and whitefish offers a wide range of high-quality fly fishing. The river lies east of the Cascade Mountains and runs mostly north from Little Lava Lake into the Columbia River east of the town of The Dalles. From Crane Prairie Reservoir, the Deschutes is a relatively small, meandering stream. From Wickiup Reservoir on it becomes a full-flowing big river. The majority of the quality fishing is on this part.

Fishing access is good for a river of this size. Along the banks there are paved roads, gravel roads, railroad tracks, mountain bike trails, and hiking paths. Where there is not access, float trips, guided and otherwise, are popular ways to get to prime locations. The river settings change from mature pine forests to sheer basalt canyons with desert vegetation, so a scenic trip is always a pleasant by-product of an outing on the Deschutes.

The beautiful canyon setting of the Deschutes River. Photo by John Judy.

Deschutes River redsides as large as this are commonplace on the Lower Deschutes. Photo by Justin Karnopp.

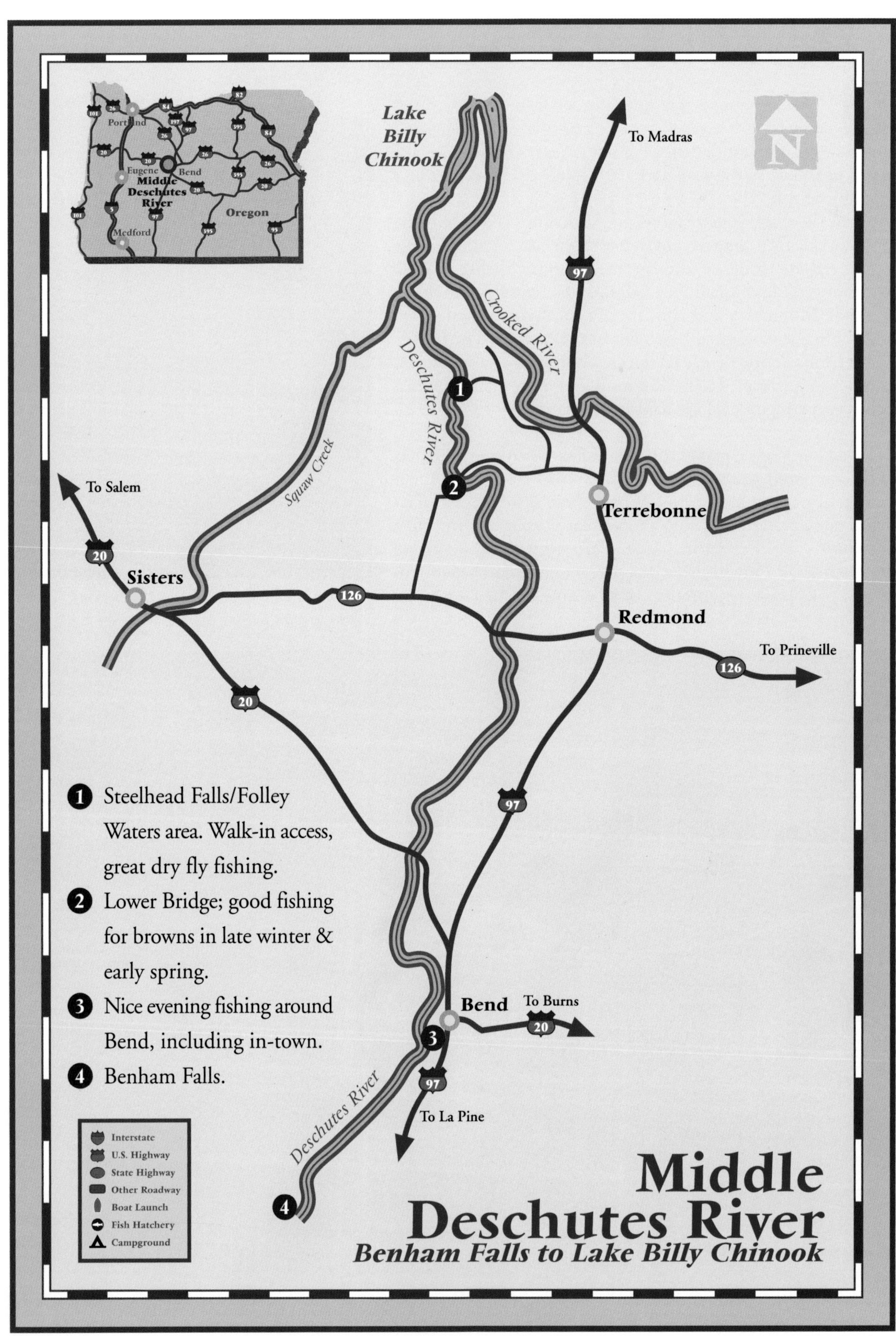
Lake
Billy
Chinook
To Madras
N
97
Crooked River
Deschutes River
Squaw Creek
To Salem
20
Sisters
126
Terrebonne
Redmond
To Prineville
126
20
97
1 Steelhead Falls/Folley Waters area. Walk-in access, great dry fly fishing.
2 Lower Bridge; good fishing for browns in late winter & early spring.
3 Nice evening fishing around Bend, including in-town.
4 Benham Falls.
Bend
To Burns
20
97
To La Pine
Deschutes River
Interstate
U.S. Highway
State Highway
Other Roadway
Boat Launch
Fish Hatchery
Campground
Middle
Deschutes River
Benham Falls to Lake Billy Chinook
Portland
Eugene
Bend
Middle
Deschutes
River
Oregon
Medford

Types of Fish

Predominantly redside rainbow trout, some bull trout, and browns. Whitefish can supply some exciting fishing.

Known Hatches

Midges, mayflies, caddis, stones, salmonflies, and terrestrials.

Equipment to Use

For Trout:

Rods: 3–6 weight, 8–10 feet in length.
Reels: Disk drag is best.
Lines: Floating and sink tip to match rod weight.
Leaders: 5X to 6X, 12 feet in length, for dries. 4X to 5X, 9 feet in length, with strike indicator, for nymphs.
Wading: Wading is always a challenge here. Wear chest-high waders with felt-soled wading shoes or stream cleats and take a wading staff. Use your best wading sense in the Deschutes!

Flies to Use

Dries: Adams, Elk Hair Caddis, Blue-Winged Olive, Slow Water Caddis, Henryville Special, CDC Caddis, Knock Down Dun, Clark's Stone, March Brown, Griffith's Gnat, X Caddis, Comparadun, Pale Morning Dun, Renegade, Salmonflies, and October Caddis.
Nymphs: Girdle Bug, Hare's Ear, Kaufman's Stone, Sparkle Caddis Pupa, Feather Duster, Beadhead Pheasant Tail, Prince, Brassie, October Caddis Pupa, Yellow Soft Hackle, Beadhead Serendipity.
Note: In late winter take a #14, #16, and #18 Black Stone. You can experience some exceptional brown trout fishing near Lower Bridge.

When to Fish

Trout fish whenever you can. Summer evening fishing is far and away the best time. Consider the hatches mentioned previously.

Seasons & Limits

Seasons and limits vary and are subject to frequent changes. Consult the Oregon Department of Fish & Wildlife regulations or a local fly shop before fishing. Fishing for trout on the upper and middle sections is from the end of April through the fall.

Nearby Fly Fishing

You can fish a section of the Warm Springs River, adjacent to the Kahneeta Hot Springs resort, with the proper tribal permit.

Accommodations & Services

Upper River: Lodging, food, and gasoline are available at South Twin Lake, Sunriver, and La Pine.
Middle River: Resorts, motels, and all supplies are available from Bend to Sisters to Redmond.

Rating

Harry & Jeff's Opinion: We've fly fished South America, Alaska, and all over the West, and the Deschutes is as good as it gets. Spectacular scenery, a good clean river, wild trout, and steelhead add up to a 10 in Oregon and the western United States.

Drift boats are used for transportation, but you have to get out of the boat to fish all of the Deschutes.

This is a match-the-hatch river where you'll find a full range of midges, mayflies, caddis, stones, and terrestrials. From late April to October, use various nymphs for trout. Dry fly action picks up in mid-May and runs through October. From late May through mid-June catch the salmonfly frenzy, then an exceptional caddis and mayfly hatch lasts through September. In October small mayflies, caddis, and midges often bring feeding trout to the surface. When in doubt, consult a local fly shop for current activity.

The Deschutes summer-run steelhead is a world-class fish! The popularity of fly fishing for them has increased greatly in the last few years. Because fly angling for these amazing fish is somewhat different than trout angling, a special page and map of the lower river and steelhead section of the Deschutes are presented after this overview section.

The three maps of the Deschutes divide the river into broad sections: upper, middle, and lower. In general, the upper section of the Deschutes runs amid ponderosa forests and meanders through the resort of Sunriver. The middle section flows through the city of Bend, through the Crooked River Ranch subdivision, into and out of Lake Billy Chinook and Lake Simtustus, and to Sherars Falls. The lower river begins at Sherars Falls, where the river makes a dramatic, unnavigable, 25-foot drop and eventually joins the mighty Columbia River. The steelhead map covers fishing this lower portion of the river.

Pete Chadwell with a colorful rainbow from the "Folley Waters" section of the Middle Deschutes. Photo by Eric Dunne.

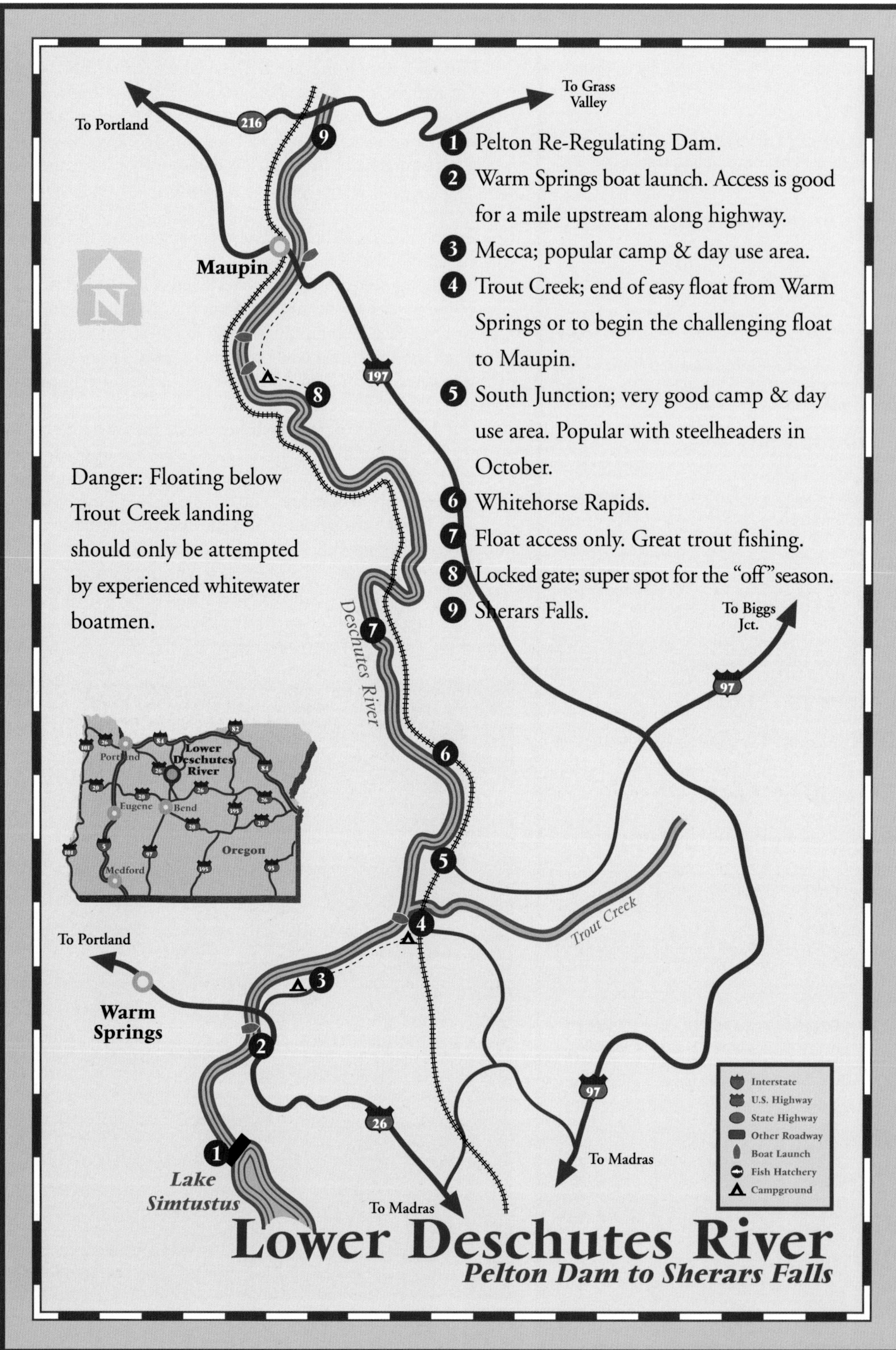

To Portland
To Grass Valley
216
9
Maupin
N
197
8
1 Pelton Re-Regulating Dam.
2 Warm Springs boat launch. Access is good for a mile upstream along highway.
3 Mecca; popular camp & day use area.
4 Trout Creek; end of easy float from Warm Springs or to begin the challenging float to Maupin.
5 South Junction; very good camp & day use area. Popular with steelheaders in October.
6 Whitehorse Rapids.
7 Float access only. Great trout fishing.
8 Locked gate; super spot for the "off" season.
9 Sherars Falls.
Danger: Floating below Trout Creek landing should only be attempted by experienced whitewater boatmen.
To Biggs Jct.
Deschutes River
7
97
6
Lower Deschutes River
Portland
Eugene
Bend
Medford
Oregon
5
Trout Creek
4
To Portland
3
Warm Springs
2
26
97
1
Lake Simtustus
To Madras
To Madras
Interstate
U.S. Highway
State Highway
Other Roadway
Boat Launch
Fish Hatchery
Campground
Lower Deschutes River
Pelton Dam to Sherars Falls

A bright Deschutes River steelhead ready for release. Photo by John Judy.

Deschutes Steelhead

Steelhead, coming from the ocean and up the mighty Columbia River, start arriving in the Deschutes in mid-July. Many local newspapers publish fish count information, or call the Oregon Department of Fish & Wildlife at (503) 872–5263. Check these counts first. When they reach 1,000 steelhead (or more) a day over Bonneville Dam it's time. By the way, many of these steelhead are Idaho hatchery fish that detour into the Deschutes every season. It's believed they stray from the warm waters in the Columbia River to the cooler waters in the Deschutes. Now that's a wrong turn on a long trip.

The downstream swing technique works best. Steelhead come up to flies just below or at the surface, so use a floating line. When the water temperature or level changes, however, steelhead tend to hunker down. A sink-tip or weighted fly may work best under these conditions. Some anglers bounce nymph-style patterns on the river bottom during these conditions. Steelhead often hold in different water than do trout. Fish tailouts or runs that have structure such as boulders or ledges.

The beautiful canyon setting of the Deschutes River. Photo by Brian O'Keefe.

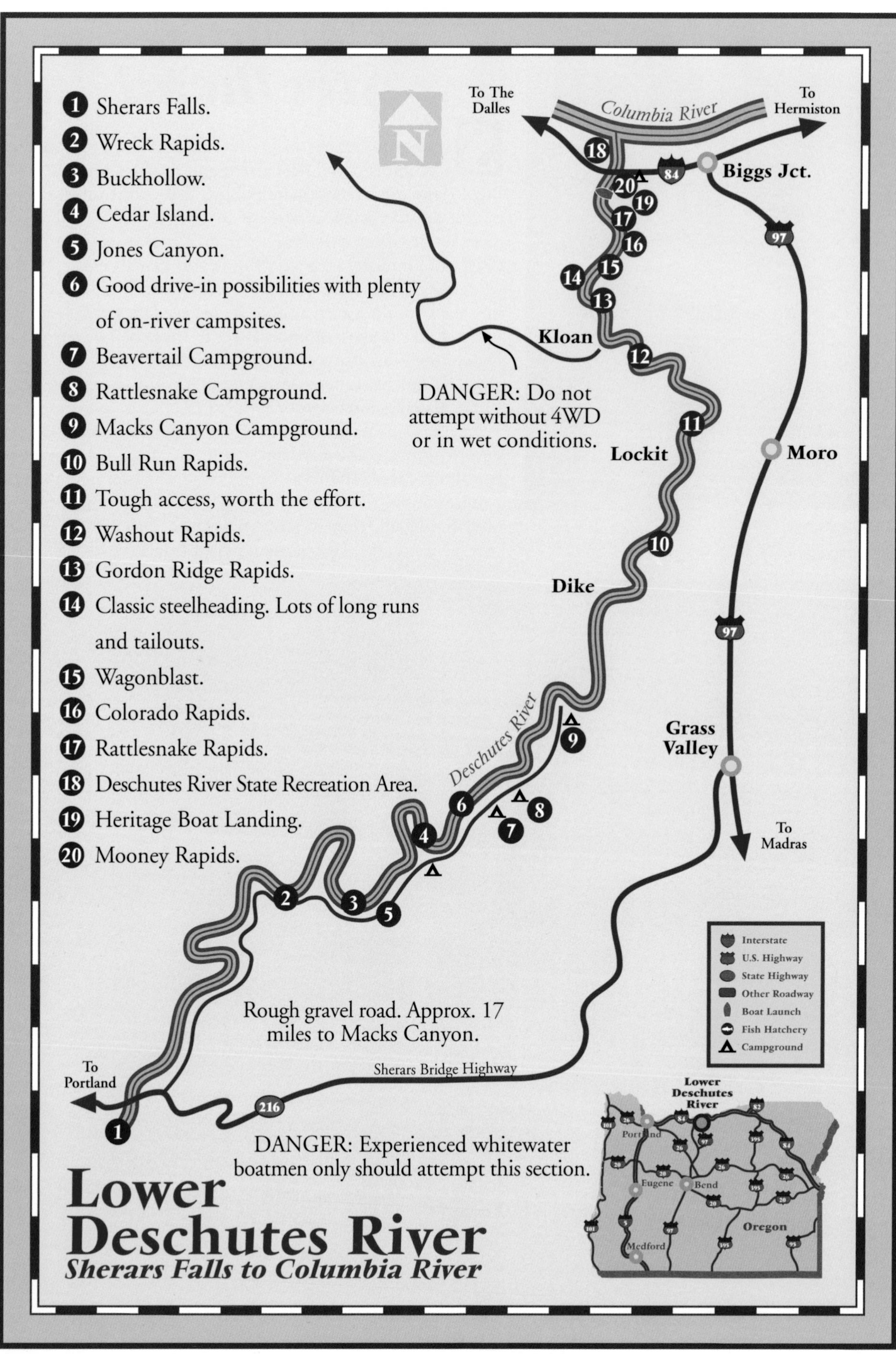

1 Sherars Falls.
2 Wreck Rapids.
3 Buckhollow.
4 Cedar Island.
5 Jones Canyon.
6 Good drive-in possibilities with plenty of on-river campsites.
7 Beavertail Campground.
8 Rattlesnake Campground.
9 Macks Canyon Campground.
10 Bull Run Rapids.
11 Tough access, worth the effort.
12 Washout Rapids.
13 Gordon Ridge Rapids.
14 Classic steelheading. Lots of long runs and tailouts.
15 Wagonblast.
16 Colorado Rapids.
17 Rattlesnake Rapids.
18 Deschutes River State Recreation Area.
19 Heritage Boat Landing.
20 Mooney Rapids.
To The Dalles
Columbia River
To Hermiston
Biggs Jct.
84
97
Kloan
DANGER: Do not attempt without 4WD or in wet conditions.
Lockit
Moro
Dike
Deschutes River
Grass Valley
To Madras
Interstate
U.S. Highway
State Highway
Other Roadway
Boat Launch
Fish Hatchery
Campground
Rough gravel road. Approx. 17 miles to Macks Canyon.
Sherars Bridge Highway
To Portland
216
Lower Deschutes River
Portland
Eugene
Bend
Medford
Oregon
DANGER: Experienced whitewater boatmen only should attempt this section.
Lower Deschutes River
Sherars Falls to Columbia River

Types of Fish

Predominantly hatchery-reared steelhead, which have one or more fins clipped for identification. Current regulations allow you to keep hatchery fish only. Let the wild ones go.

Equipment to Use

Rods: 6–8 weight, 9–10 feet in length. Spey, 6–9 weight, 11½–15 feet in length.
Reels: Disk drag with 100–200 yards of backing.
Lines: Steelhead taper or WF floating, 10–13- foot type III sink tip, 200 grain sink tip.
Wading: Use chest-high neoprene or breathable waders, felt-soled boots, and cleats for slippery rocks and swift currents. Regulars use a wading staff or personal flotation device.

Flies to Use

Attractor patterns: Sparsely tied "low water" patterns in purple, black, and orange are best. Purple Peril, Freight Train, Green-Butt Skunk, Skunk, Red Wing Blackbird, Mack's Canyon.
Weighted Flies: Purple Flash, Articulated Leech, Lead Eye Egg-Sucking Woolly Bugger, Girdle Bug, Beadhead Prince.

When to Fish

From Sherars Falls upstream to Pelton Dam, steelheading is best in the fall. The 44 river miles from Sherars Falls to the mouth is best fly fished from late July through October. Usually late July through October is best up to Macks Canyon. August through November is great from Macks Canyon to Sherars Falls. In late September and October, Sherars Falls to Warm Springs is best. Steelheading at dawn can be the key to success, though any time the direct sun is off the water is a prime time to fish for steelhead with a fly.

Seasons & Limits

The steelhead season on the Deschutes begins in late April and ends December 31. Anglers possessing a steelhead tag may take 2 adipose fin-clipped steelhead per day. Wild steelhead (those with intact adipose fin) must be released.

Accommodations & Services

If fishing up from the mouth, you can find motels and all services in Biggs Junction and The Dalles (with a wider choice of restaurants in The Dalles). If fishing above Macks Canyon, food, services, and motels are found in Grass Valley, Maupin, Madras, Bend, Redmond, and Sisters. Campsites are marked all along the river and at the mouth. Kloan is the only access to the 25 miles of water from Macks Canyon to the mouth. Take everything you need into this section. No facilities are available of any type.

Rating

Jeff's Opinion: Since 1991, when Harry Teel introduced me to this fishery, it's become one of my favorites. My wife and I consider steelhead our favorite game fish and, come July, we can't wait to go to the lower Deschutes. If you can wade, cast 50 feet, and mend line, you can probably catch a steelhead here. Depending on the run of Steelhead, at least a 6. In a good year, 9 to 10.

Floating from Buckhollow to Heritage Boat Landing is a three- to six-day trip. However you can take out at one of the campgrounds above Macks Canyon and make a one- or two-day trip out of it. The *Handbook to the Deschutes River Canyon* is invaluable!

From the Columbia, at Deschutes River State Recreation Area and Heritage Landing, many fly fishers hike up either side of the river. Riding a mountain bike up the east-side trail is also popular. A less arduous trip is via jet boat up through the powerful whitewater. Either way, you are entering a prime summer steelhead area.

From central Oregon take Highway 97 north to Biggs Junction. Highway 197 accesses the town of Maupin. Highway 216, out of Grass Valley, goes to the Sherars Falls area. For direct vehicle access, use the road from Sherars Falls to Macks Canyon. The 17 miles of gravel road follows plenty of water, has many turnouts, and is a good bet for a day trip. Better yet, pitch a tent at one of the many Bureau of Land Management sites. Remember your alarm clock and rise early so you're assured of a portion of river before sunup.

A two-handed spey rod is a great way to cover the water when steelheading on the Deschutes. Photo by John Judy.

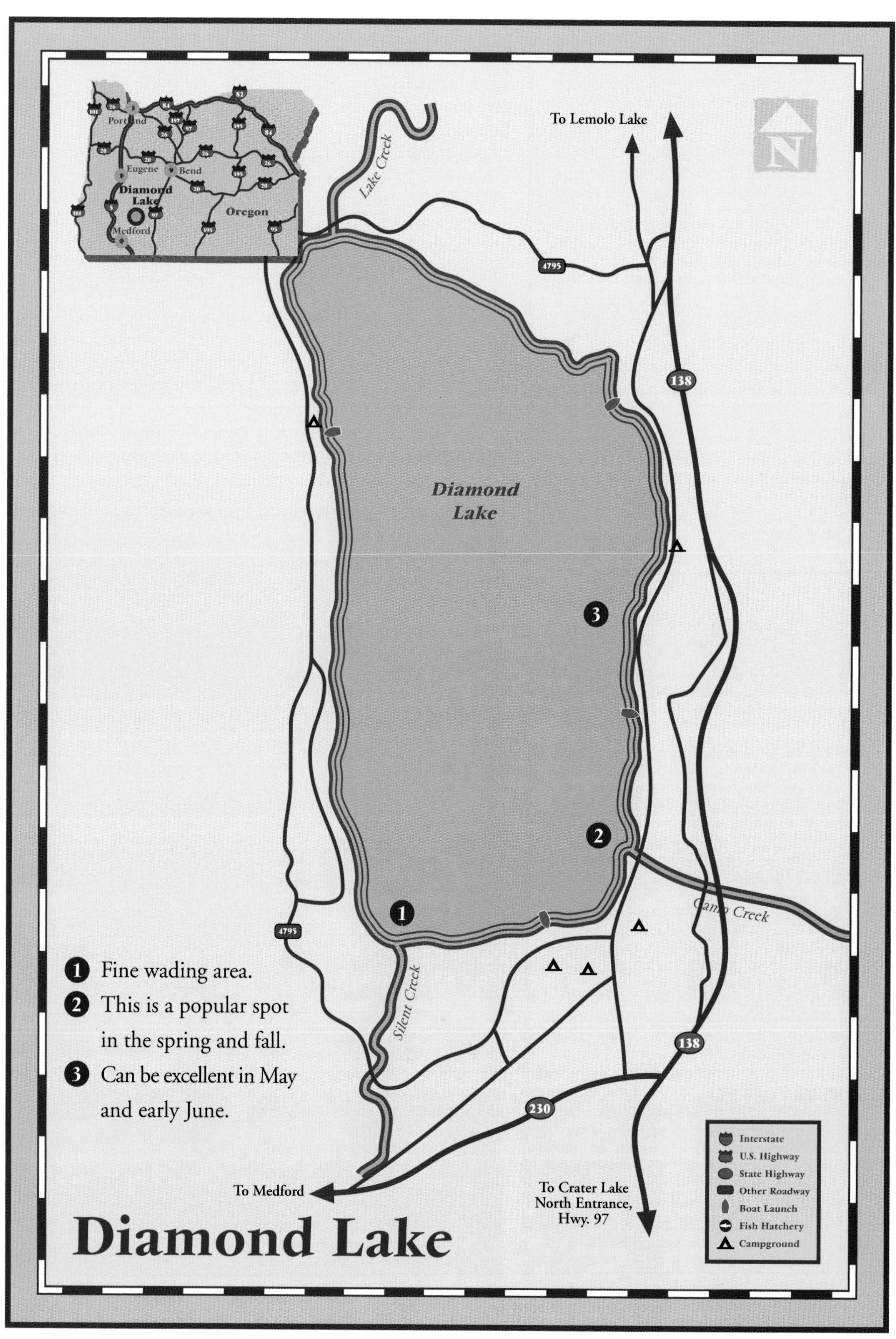

1 Fine wading area.

2 This is a popular spot in the spring and fall.

3 Can be excellent in May and early June.

Diamond Lake

Diamond Lake

Diamond Lake may be the most productive lake in the state for trout food and quick-growing rainbows. Fish over five pounds are taken each year. People tend to think of Diamond as a trolling and baitfishing lake, but you can also have great fly fishing action, depending on the chub activity. The Oregon Department of Fish & Wildlife poisoned unwanted fish in 1999. Healthy Williamson rainbow trout were reintroduced, which provided thousands of 18- to 20-inch brutes.

Then, by the late summer of 2001, the illegally introduced tui chub population again grew out of control. This trash fish, up to four inches long, ate the microscopic zooplankton that normally keep the lake's algae in check. The uncontrolled blue-green algae then dominated and released toxins that led to the lake's closure.

When this edition went to press, the lake was back to near normal with about 100,000 catchable fish planted each year, including chinook salmon, Eagle Lake rainbow trout, and about 15,000 two-pound rainbow trout. So, now back to the fly fishing.

Though it's more than three miles long and just under two miles wide, fly anglers should consider float tubing Diamond Lake. Look for areas 10 to 20 feet deep, or try the waters along drop-offs on the western and eastern shores. Trolling and the sink-and-retrieve nymph or streamer techniques are effective. Use lots of line. Always look out for passing boats, which should be going 10 mph or less during fishing season. This said, don't forget that wading can be very productive here, too.

Diamond, at 5,182 feet in elevation, offers a wonderful mountain setting with views of nearby Mt. Bailey and Mt. Thielsen. The heavily forested area has plenty of campgrounds and visitor facilities and is a good place for family camping, fishing, and hiking. Crater Lake National Park, a short drive away, is a "must-see" while in Oregon.

Diamond Lake is in far southeastern Douglas County, well marked and accessed from Highway 138. It's most easily accessed from the east via Highway 97 and Highway 138. From the south and west use Highways 230 and 138.

Mt. Thielsen (9,182 feet) looms over Diamond Lake. Photo by Pete Chadwell.

Types of Fish

Chinook salmon and rainbow trout, 10 to 24 inches, averaging one pound plus.

Known Hatches

Midges and mayflies hatch in the spring.

Equipment to Use

Rods: 6–7 weight, 9–9½ feet in length.
Reels: Mechanical and palm drag.
Lines: Floating line to match rod size.
Leaders: 4X or 5X, 9 feet in length.
Wading: Use chest-high waders and boots for float tubing and wading.

Flies to Use

Dries: Midge, Comparadun, Adams, Blue Dun.
Nymphs: Leech, Damsel, Hare's Ear, Chironomid.

When to Fish

Best when the ice thaws in late April and fish start their spring spawning. Fishing can remain good through May and sometimes into early June. It picks up again in September and October. The lake fishes well nearly all day long.

Seasons & Limits

Open from late April through the end of October. A 10-fish-per-day limit has been in effect, but check exact dates and limits in the current Oregon Department of Fish & Wildlife regulations.

Accommodations & Services

Good campgrounds are along the lake. Diamond Lake Lodge has cabins, food, stores, and gas. There are several boat ramps.

Rating

Harry's Opinion: Diamond Lake can be one of the finest lake fisheries in the West, offering an opportunity to catch plenty of quality trout. For all types of fishing, it is a 9. For fly fishing, it's a 7.5.

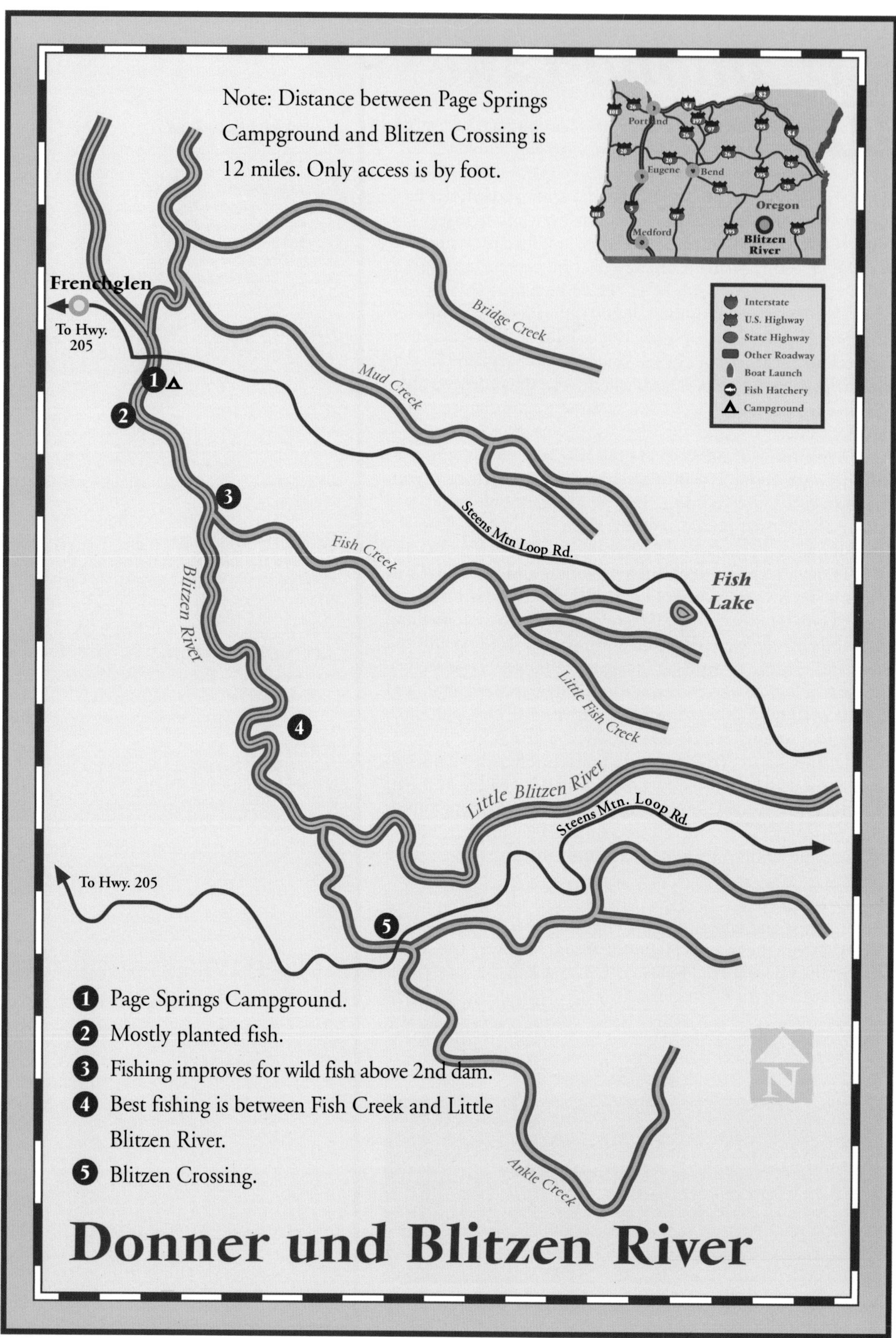

Note: Distance between Page Springs Campground and Blitzen Crossing is 12 miles. Only access is by foot.
Portland
Eugene
Bend
Medford
Oregon
Blitzen River
Interstate
U.S. Highway
State Highway
Other Roadway
Boat Launch
Fish Hatchery
Campground
Frenchglen
To Hwy. 205
Bridge Creek
Mud Creek
Steens Mtn Loop Rd.
Fish Creek
Fish Lake
Blitzen River
Little Fish Creek
Little Blitzen River
Steens Mtn. Loop Rd.
To Hwy. 205
Ankle Creek
N
1 Page Springs Campground.
2 Mostly planted fish.
3 Fishing improves for wild fish above 2nd dam.
4 Best fishing is between Fish Creek and Little Blitzen River.
5 Blitzen Crossing.
Donner und Blitzen River

Donner und Blitzen River

I'm one happy person when I'm in this remote section of Oregon and fishing the Donner und Blitzen (commonly referred to as just the Blitzen). If I could design my own trout stream, I'd use the Blitzen above Page Springs Campground as a model. The river above Page Springs flows through a relatively narrow canyon that's lined with juniper and pine trees. If you like small, remote, desert streams, the Blitzen will fulfill one of your fly fishing fantasies. The Blitzen originates in the Steens Mountain range, one of the most scenic regions in Oregon.

Donner und Blitzen, German for "thunder and lightning," refers to a single river. The name originated when Army troops who were crossing the river in 1864 encountered a big thunderstorm. The storms over the Steens Mountain area can certainly get your attention, so bring along rain gear, even in the summer.

This is a wonderful trout stream, but it requires lots of walking to get to the best fishing. Hardy rainbows are your reward. Because you will do a lot of walking to find these fish, make sure your wading equipment is comfortable and fits properly.

Depending on the time of year you fish the Blitzen, you'll need to adapt your pattern selection to what's happening on the river. There is one fly I've found that fishes well, regardless of the time of year: Royal Wulff #14.

The Blitzen is located about 65 miles south of Burns, Oregon, near the community of Frenchglen. Highway 205 from Burns to Frenchglen is paved. From Frenchglen to Page Springs Campground, about three miles, the road is gravel. Another approach is via the East Canal access road on the Malheur Refuge. It is open to non-motorized traffic only.

An angler working a run on the Donner und Blitzen. Photo by Brian O'Keefe.

Types of Fish

Rainbow trout, generally from 8 to 14 inches, although fish up to 20 inches are taken on a regular basis.

Known Hatches

Mayflies, caddis and terrestrials.

Equipment to Use

Rods: 1–5 weight, 6½–9 feet in length.
Reels: Palm or mechanical drag.
Lines: Floating to match rod weight.
Leaders: 4X and 5X leaders, 9 feet in length.
Wading: Here's what I do when fishing the Blitzen: I take felt-soled wading boots (which I normally use with my chest waders), put on neoprene socks, and wade in my everyday fishing pants. Yes, I get wet up to my thighs, but on a hot day in Donner und Blitzen Canyon, the cool water is a welcome relief. Lightweight nylon hippers with wading boots are also easy to wear for walking.

Flies to Use

Dries: Royal Wulff #14, Comparadun, Elk Hair Caddis, Adams, Hopper, Renegade, and Humpy.
Nymphs & Streamers: Prince, Hare's Ear, Sculpin, Pheasant Tail and Beadheads, Woolly Bugger, Muddler.

When to Fish

Fishing the Blitzen from mid-July through October has been best for me. April and May fishing can be OK but, depending on runoff, the river can be high and out of shape. Fishing in the late afternoon and evening is generally most productive.

Seasons & Limits

Generally, this is an April through October fly fishing stream. Check the Oregon Department of Fish & Wildlife regulations for exact dates and limits.

Accommodations & Services

Frenchglen has a small hotel with food service, a store, gas, and not much else. At Page Springs, there is a wonderful Bureau of Land Management campground. A private trailer park near Page Springs Campground has limited supplies and rents trailers for overnight accommodations.

Rating

Harry's Opinion: The Blitzen is a delicate resource that needs our protection. It can stand a reasonable amount of fishing and recreational pressure if we all practice intelligent conservation. I strongly recommend that you practice catch and release on this stream. Remote, good trout, a strong 6.5.

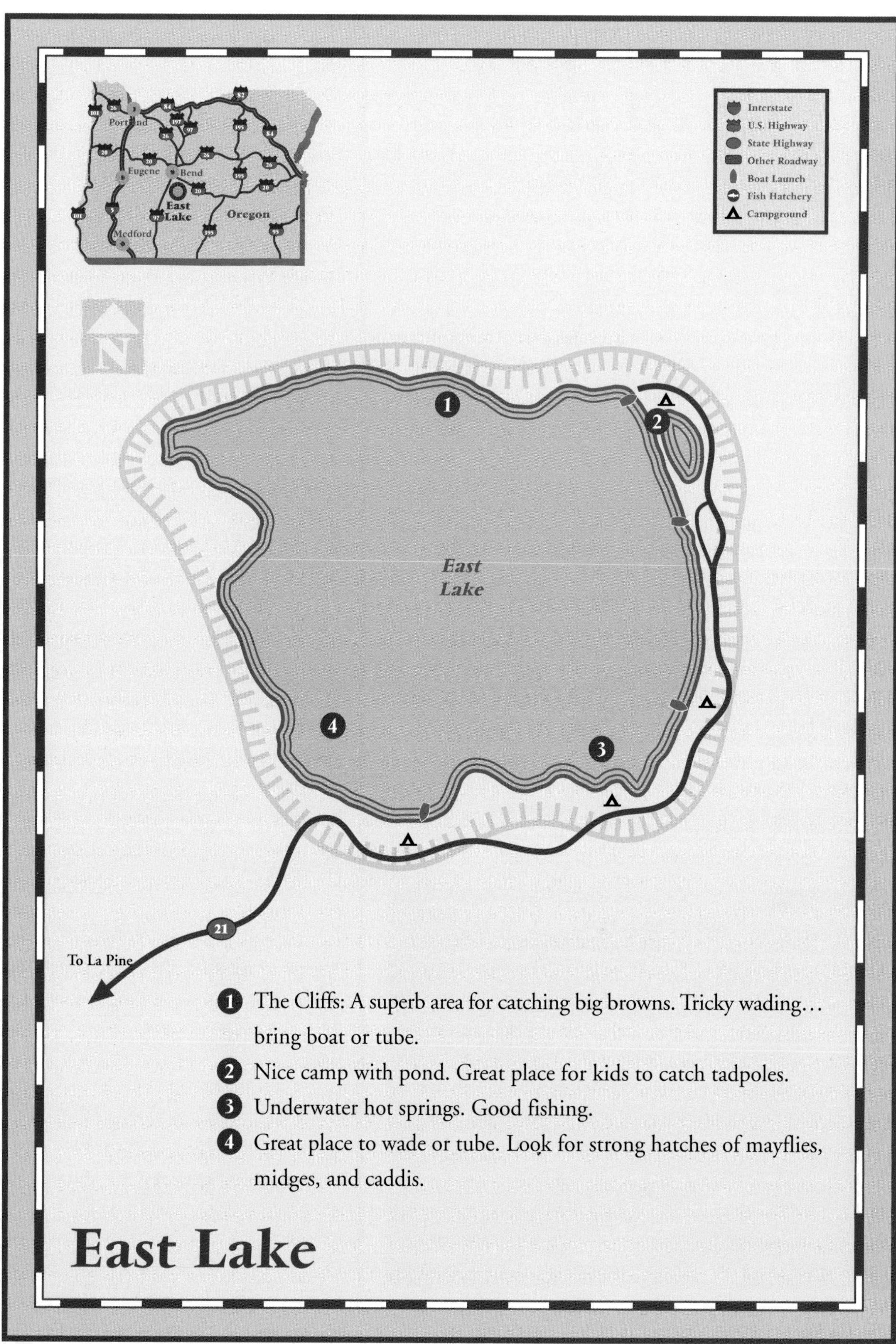

1. The Cliffs: A superb area for catching big browns. Tricky wading… bring boat or tube.
2. Nice camp with pond. Great place for kids to catch tadpoles.
3. Underwater hot springs. Good fishing.
4. Great place to wade or tube. Look for strong hatches of mayflies, midges, and caddis.

East Lake

East Lake

Fly fishing possibilities are almost limitless at East Lake. This combines with the short drive from central Oregon's major cities to make East Lake a favorite still water. A roundabout reason for catch and release angling has helped this fishery. A few years back, higher than average levels of mercury were found in East Lake fish. The Health Department recommended not eating them. Almost overnight, East Lake transformed into a great catch and release lake, and sizes and numbers of fish improved dramatically.

East Lake is about 1,000 acres and more than 170 feet deep in the middle. Water stays cool at this elevation, even in summer. Unlike its nearby cousin, Paulina Lake (541-536-2240), East has vast, weedy, and shallow shoreline areas. Scuds, leeches, chironomids, mayflies, caddis, and damsels grow in these warmer areas.

Casting for an assortment of feisty fish is exciting. In October, fish streamers for big fish. Wading, boating, and float tubing are all effective methods. Unless you have a motorboat, fish areas close to one of the boat launches or campgrounds.

East Lake has some very good campgrounds. For families with kids, try Cinderhill, where there's a small pond loaded with tadpoles and frogs. East Lake can have a bear or two wandering around. They don't usually bother people, but use common sense and don't leave food out overnight. If you have time, take the drive up to Paulina Peak. What a view!

East Lake is easy to get to. From Bend, go south 22 miles on Highway 97, then 20 miles east up Road 21 (Paulina East Lake Road). East Lake is at 6,380 feet in elevation, so snow is possible even in the summer.

A rainbow trout from East Lake about to be released. Photo by Brian O'Keefe.

Types of Fish

Rainbow, brown, and a few brook trout, Atlantic salmon.

Known Hatches

Callibaetis, Chironomid, long-horned caddis, damselflies, scuds, crayfish, forage fish, and leeches.

Equipment to Use

Rods: 3–6 weight, 8½–10 feet in length.
Reels: Click or disk drag.
Lines: Floating, intermediate, types 2 to 4 for the deep areas.
Leaders: 3X to 6X, 9–15 feet in length, 7½ feet in length for sinking lines.
Wading: Use neoprene or breathable waders and felt-soled boots. Use cleats in The Cliffs area. A boat or float tube is best.

Flies to Use

Dries: Parachute Adams, Callibaetis Spinner, Comparadun, Timberline Emerger, Suspender Midge, Para-Midge, Griffith's Gnat, Black Elk Hair Caddis, X Caddis, Adult Damsel, Ant, Beetle, and Float-N-Fool.
Nymphs & Streamers: Scud, Pheasant Tail, Gold Ribbed Hare's Ear, Soft Hackle Hare's Ear, Beadhead Prince, Beadhead Leech, Woolly Bugger, Carey Special, Damsel, Zonker, Marabou Muddler, Sculpin Bugger, Crayfish Bunny Matuka.

When to Fish

From mid to late June through October 1, hatches are prime. Fishing is usually best in the late mornings and evenings.

Seasons & Limits

Open from the last Saturday in April to October 31. Ice can be locked in until June. Check at a fly shop for early-season fishing conditions. Most fishing techniques are permitted. Limits on fish vary, so consult a local fly shop or the Oregon Department of Fish & Game regulations.

Nearby Fly Fishing

Paulina Lake.

Accommodations & Services

Good campsites. East Lake Resort has cabins and a restaurant (541-536-2230). All other services are available in La Pine, Sunriver, and Bend.

Rating

Jeff's Opinion: The 1990s helped East Lake, and it is now one of the best fly fishing lakes in central Oregon. Continue to practice catch and release and East will continue to be hot. Definitely an 8.

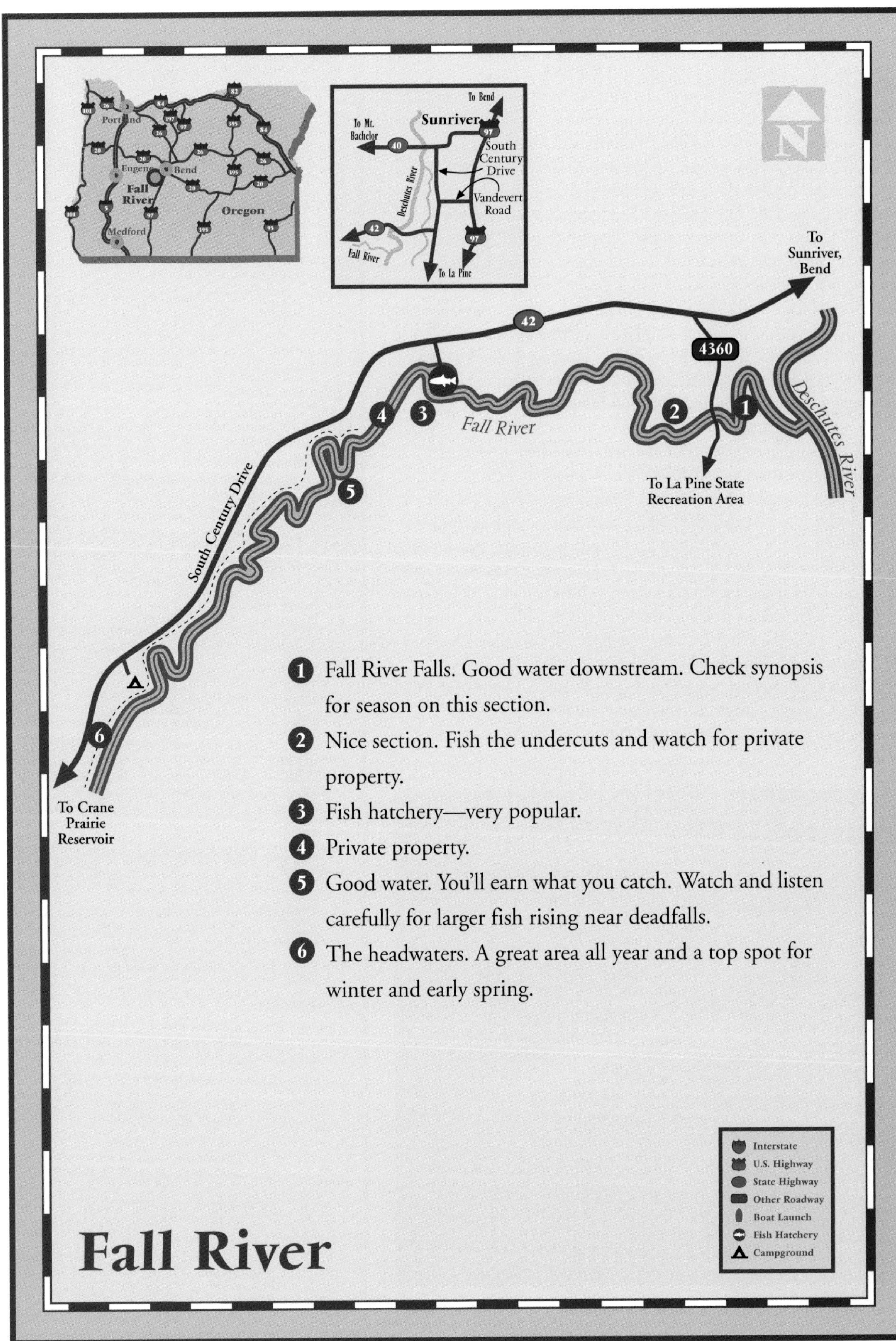

1. Fall River Falls. Good water downstream. Check synopsis for season on this section.
2. Nice section. Fish the undercuts and watch for private property.
3. Fish hatchery—very popular.
4. Private property.
5. Good water. You'll earn what you catch. Watch and listen carefully for larger fish rising near deadfalls.
6. The headwaters. A great area all year and a top spot for winter and early spring.

Fall River

Fall River

Fall River is only about 25 miles southwest of Bend and is readily accessible off South Century Drive. Its proximity to the Sunriver resort and the towns of Bend and La Pine make it a popular destination for local fly fishers, especially those who prefer rivers. The water upstream from the falls is open year-round, which is a pleasure for winter anglers or Mt. Bachelor skiers looking for diversion from the slopes.

Fall River is approximately 10 miles long, its origin being a spring below Wickiup Reservoir. It flows through a pine forest and ultimately empties into the Deschutes River between Sunriver and La Pine. You'll like the topographic features of the area, from the gentle, rolling hills of the pine forest to the volcanic cinder buttes that are scattered across the landscape. During mosquito season, be sure to have a good repellent.

The river is very clear and cold. Good casting presentations are important. Keep a low profile along Fall River so you don't spook the fish. Fall River has a lot of blown-down timber. Pay attention to these areas; they provide cover and pools for the larger trout. Polarized glasses will help you spot and catch more fish in these spots. These fish are usually dining on midges and mayflies. Caddis and small stoneflies are also productive patterns. Weights are not permitted so use Woolly Buggers and Beadhead Nymphs in a dropper setup.

Deadfalls litter the Fall River and provide excellent cover for some large trout. Photo by Brian O'Keefe.

Types of Fish

Rainbow, brook, and brown trout. The majority run 8 to 12 inches, but keep an eye out for bigger fish.

Known Hatches

Caddis, midges, mayflies, and small stoneflies.

Equipment to Use

Rods: 1–5 weight, 6–9 feet in length.
Reels: Palm drag is fine.
Lines: Floating line to match rod weight.
Leaders: 5X to 7X, 9–15 feet in length, depending on where you're fishing and the weather.
Wading: Breathable waders with felt-soled wading boots. Hippers are okay on hot summer days.

Flies to Use

Dries: Adams, Renegade, Comparadun, Pale Morning Dun, Blue-Winged Olive, Knock Down Dun, Captive Dun, Slow Water Caddis, CDC & Elk Hair Caddis, Henryville Special, Griffith's Gnat, Palomino, Ant Stimulator, Humpy, Madam X, Para-Hopper.
Nymphs: Pheasant Tail, Prince, Brassie, Serendipity, Hare's Ear, Sparkle Pupa, Zug Bug, Soft Hackle, also all in beadhead.
Streamers: Zonker, Woolly Bugger, Mickey Finn.

When to Fish

Fishing holds up pretty well all year because of the Oregon Department of Fish & Wildlife stocking program. Most Fall River enthusiasts like late June, July, and August. Evening hours generally produce the best results.

Seasons & Limits

Artificial flies only, weights (on line or leader) prohibited. The river is open from April 26 through September 30 below the falls and all year upstream from the falls. Watch for private property. Check the Oregon Department of Fish & Wildlife regulations or ask at a nearby fly shop for exact dates and limits.

Accommodations & Services

There are good campsites along the river. Sunriver, Bend, and La Pine have lodging and are within a half-hour drive. Stores, restaurants, gas, and groceries are also available in these locations.

Rating

Jeff's Opinion: This spring-fed creek offers consistent, year-round fly fishing. You'll like the beauty of the Fall River. It takes good presentation (aided by polarized glasses). If you enjoy light equipment and delicate casts, put Fall River on your "must-fish" list. It is a high-end 6.

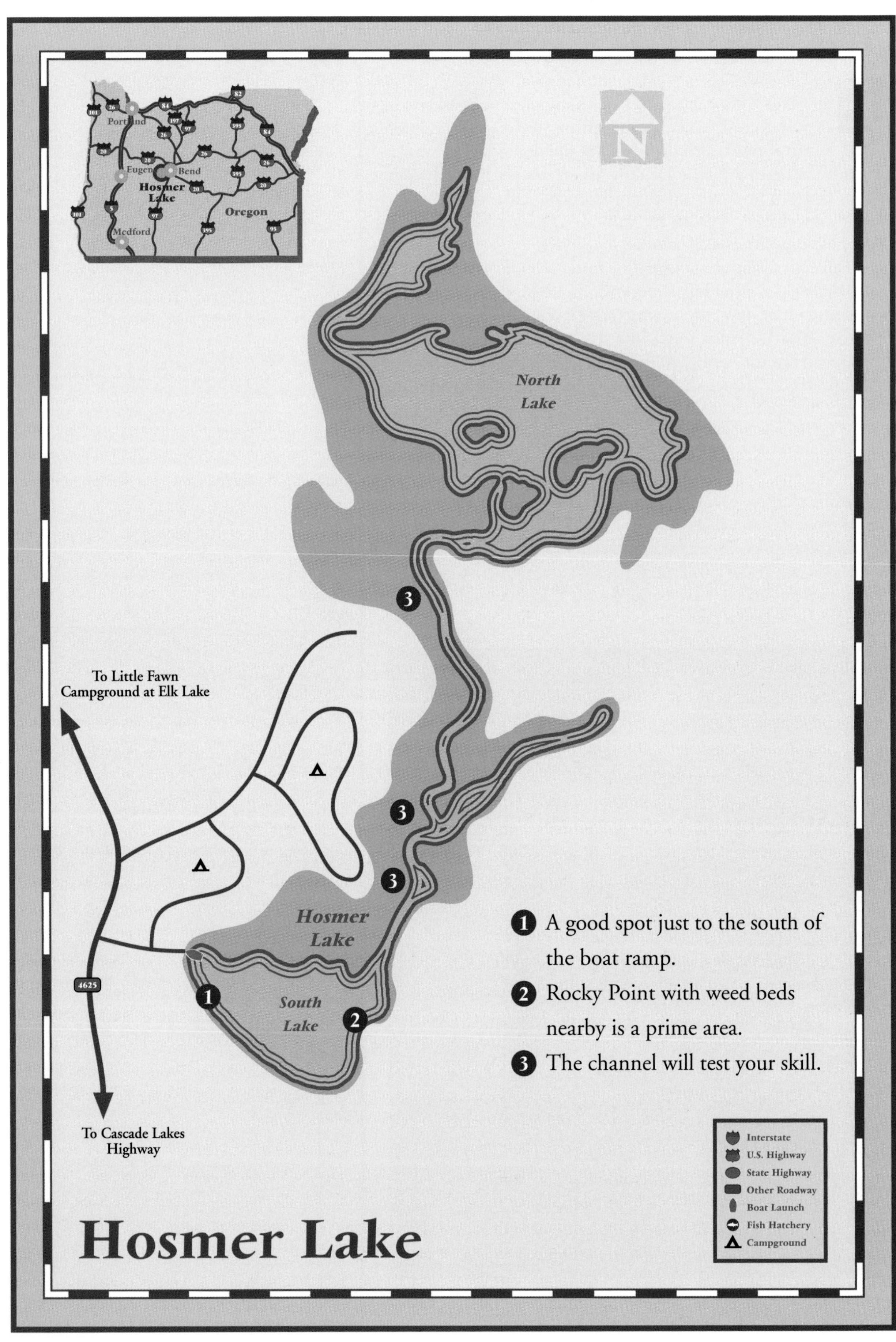
Portland
Eugene
Bend
Hosmer Lake
Oregon
Medford
North Lake
To Little Fawn Campground at Elk Lake
Hosmer Lake
South Lake
4625
To Cascade Lakes Highway
1 A good spot just to the south of the boat ramp.
2 Rocky Point with weed beds nearby is a prime area.
3 The channel will test your skill.
Interstate
U.S. Highway
State Highway
Other Roadway
Boat Launch
Fish Hatchery
Campground
Hosmer Lake

Hosmer Lake

Hosmer is one of the most remarkable fly-fishing-only, catch and release fisheries in the state of Oregon. Feisty landlocked Atlantic salmon and large, beautiful brook trout make this figure-eight-shaped lake a real favorite of central Oregon fly fishers. Views of the snowcapped peaks make for one of the most scenic still waters for fly fishing in these parts.

The 6- to 20-foot-deep lake has large weed beds along much of the shoreline and extensive shallows where a rich food supply helps grow the husky, good fighting fish. A shallow channel connecting the two main sections usually contains large brookies cruising the feeding lanes. Watching these fish is often as fun as figuring out how to catch them. Fish the channel, the weed beds along the west side, or the east and south shores of the larger (northern) lake.

Most of Hosmer Lake can be fished from a float tube. Boats help with covering the entire area. Wading is possible but limited due to the very soft, muddy shallows. Remember that there is no trolling (i.e., fishing from a motor-propelled craft when the motor is running).

Hosmer is located in Deschutes County, about 35 miles southwest of Bend, Oregon. Take Century Drive (Forest Highway 46) toward Elk Lake Resort and look for signs.

South Sister (10,360 feet) looks on as an angler hunts for Atlantic salmon. Photo by Brian O'Keefe.

Types of Fish

Good-quality Atlantic salmon and brook trout. Both species grow to nice sizes in this food-rich environment.

Known Hatches

Mayflies, caddis, and midges.

Equipment to Use

Rods: 4–7 weight, 8–9 feet in length.
Reels: Mechanical and palm drag.
Lines: Floating lines matched to rod weight.
Leaders: 4X to 6X, 9–15 feet in length. Fluorocarbon is great.
Wading: To fish Hosmer properly, you'll need a boat, canoe, or float tube. There are restrictions on motors, so be sure to consult the Oregon Department of Fish & Wildlife regulations. For float tubes, bring chest-high neoprene waders with felt-soled wading shoes and fins.

Flies to Use

Dries: Parachute Adams, Comparadun, Parachute Caddis, Goddard Caddis, Tom Thumb, Palomino Midge, Century Drive Midge, Timberline Emerger, Callibaetis.
Nymphs: Leech, Stovepipe, Damsel, Scud, Carey Special, Beadhead Serendipity, Zug Bug, Pheasant Tail, Cates Turkey, Water Boatman, Kokanee Candy, Top Banana.

When to Fish

Opinions are mixed: Some like June and July, while others prefer late September and October. I feel both are good times, with good opportunities to take nice sized fish. Most Hosmer fly fishers agree that evening is the best time of day for any kind of fly fishing.

Seasons & Limits

The season opens in late April and continues through the end of October. For exact dates and limits, consult the current Oregon Department of Fish & Wildlife regulations or a local fly shop.

Nearby Fly Fishing

Hosmer is about ten miles from Crane Prairie Reservoir, another central Oregon favorite.

Accommodations & Services

There are good campgrounds at the lake. The nearest accommodations, food and gas, are located at Elk Lake Resort, just a few miles away. A full range of services is available in Bend, Sunriver, and La Pine.

Rating

Harry's Opinion: Hosmer is a very scenic lake with lots of wildlife. If you're looking for a lake that will challenge your fly fishing skills, don't look any further, just head for Hosmer. A 5.5.

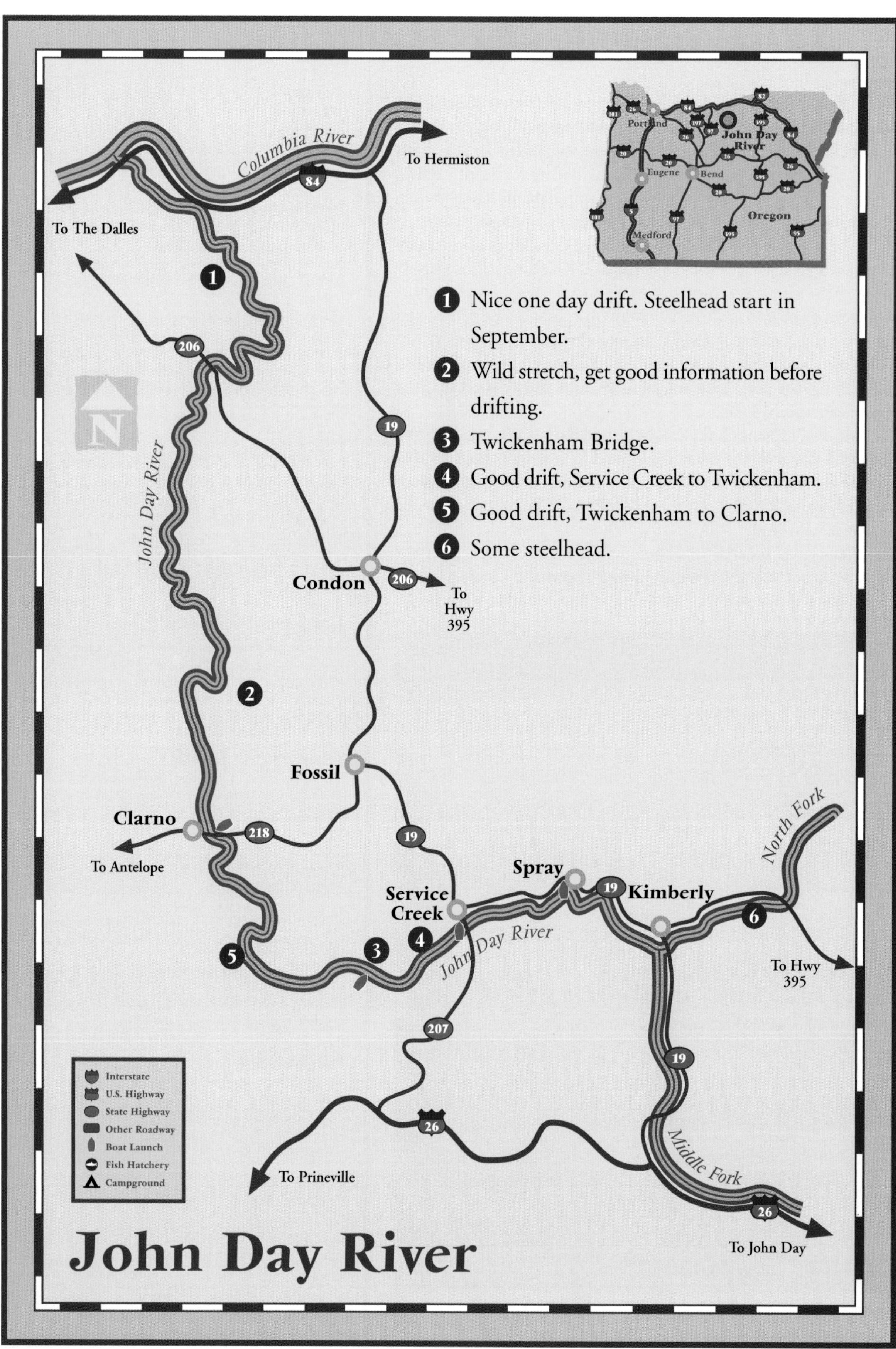
Columbia River
To Hermiston
84
To The Dalles
206
19
John Day River
Condon
206
To Hwy 395
Fossil
Clarno
218
To Antelope
19
Spray
19
Kimberly
Service Creek
John Day River
North Fork
To Hwy 395
207
19
26
To Prineville
Middle Fork
26
To John Day
Portland
John Day River
Eugene
Bend
Oregon
Medford
1 Nice one day drift. Steelhead start in September.
2 Wild stretch, get good information before drifting.
3 Twickenham Bridge.
4 Good drift, Service Creek to Twickenham.
5 Good drift, Twickenham to Clarno.
6 Some steelhead.
Interstate
U.S. Highway
State Highway
Other Roadway
Boat Launch
Fish Hatchery
Campground
John Day River

John Day River

If you like semiarid landscape, you'll fall in love with the John Day River. It is the only major stream in the Columbia drainage system in Oregon without a hydroelectric project blocking migratory fish. The 275-mile river begins in the eastern portion of central Oregon, up in the Blue Mountains. It runs north from above the town of John Day to enter the Columbia River not far from the mouth of the Deschutes. Water levels vary considerably depending on the season and the demands of agriculture. Also, much of the river runs though private property, so access can be tricky.

The John Day does offer three species of fish for the fly angler and not a lot of fishing pressure, except for the rafting crowd in early summer. Fish for smallmouth bass in well more than 70 miles of the lower river from mid-spring through summer. Steelheading is good in fall and winter from the Cottonwood area up to about Kimberly. Several years ago the Oregon Department of Fish & Wildlife biologist responsible for the John Day River drainage stated that the native steelhead run in the river was the largest in Oregon. He indicated that approximately 26,000 of these fish were observed on the spawning beds. Trout, native and hatchery, are available almost all year in the upper sections.

The more popular section, where there are lots of access points, is between Kimberly and Service Creek. For the next 100 or so miles below Service Creek access is really limited. Drifting below Clarno can be tricky.

The arid environs of the John Day River. Photo by Brian O'Keefe.

Types of Fish

Rainbow trout, steelhead, and smallmouth bass.

Known Hatches & Baitfish

Mayflies, caddis, and terrestrials.

Equipment to Use

You'll need a variety of equipment depending on the time of year. Here are general guidelines.

Bass & Trout:
Rods: 4–7 weight, 8–9 feet in length.
Reels: Palm drag or disk drag.
Lines: Floating and sink tip to match rod weight.
Leaders: 3X to 5X, 7–9 feet in length.

Steelhead:
Rods: 6–9 weight, 8–9 feet in length.
Reels: Mechanical drag.
Lines: Floating and sink tip to match rod weight.
Leaders: 1X to 3X, 7–9 feet in length.
Wading: Use chest-high neoprene or breathable waders with felt-soled wading shoes or stream cleats and a wading staff. If you are planning to float below Clarno, consult a qualified and knowledgeable guide.

Flies to Use

Your fly choice will depend on whether you are fishing for trout, bass, or steelhead. My experience suggests the following:

For Trout:
Dries: Adams, Renegade, Elk Hair Caddis, X Caddis, Humpy, Light Cahill, Blue-Winged Olive, Comparadun, Grasshopper, Foam Ant.
Nymphs & Streamers: Woolly Worm, Hare's Ear, Matuka, Muddler, Zonker, Woolly Bugger.
For Steelhead: Skunk, Green-Butt Skunk, Red Wing Blackbird, Silver Hilton.
For Bass: Surface Poppers, Sliders, and Wiggle Bugs are effective and fun. Try yellow and chartreuse first, then orange, red, white, black, brown, green, and purple, Clouser Minnow, and Near Nuff Crayfish.

When to Fish

Water flows vary dramatically, so consult a qualified guide. Fish for bass from May through August, and for steelhead in the late fall and winter months. Trout fishing is good most of the year.

Seasons & Limits

There is great variance of seasons and regulations by species and river section on the John Day. Be sure to check at a fly shop or with the Oregon Department of Fish & Wildlife in John Day (541-575-1167) for current regulations.

Accommodations & Services

Facilities are limited along the accessible length of the river. Restaurants, service stations, and groceries are located downstream from Kimberly. There are some nice campsites between Kimberly and Service Creek.

Rating

Harry's Opinion: The John Day can range from a 2 to a 6, depending on when you fish. I suggest you take the time to carefully evaluate the steelhead fishery. For trout a 2. For bass an 8. For steelhead, a strong 5.

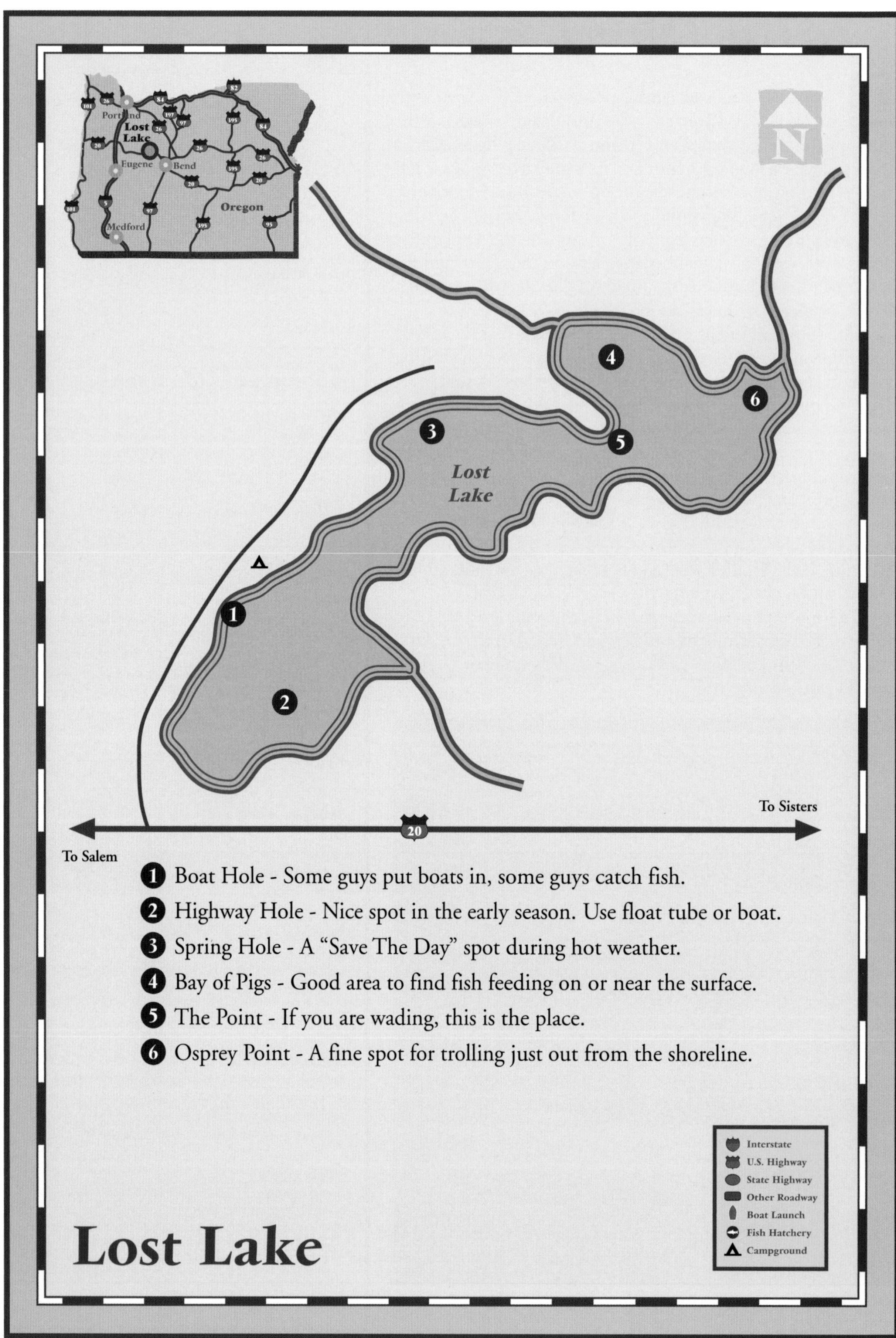

1. Boat Hole - Some guys put boats in, some guys catch fish.
2. Highway Hole - Nice spot in the early season. Use float tube or boat.
3. Spring Hole - A "Save The Day" spot during hot weather.
4. Bay of Pigs - Good area to find fish feeding on or near the surface.
5. The Point - If you are wading, this is the place.
6. Osprey Point - A fine spot for trolling just out from the shoreline.

Lost Lake

Lost Lake

Here's an excellent still-water fishery very near Sisters, Black Butte Ranch, and Camp Sherman, and hardly anyone talks about it. Lost Lake is very easy to locate and great for float tubing. If you can ignore the occasional traffic noise from the highway, you'll enjoy casting to lots of healthy trout in one of the most productive lakes in the Sisters area.

Situated in a basin below Three Fingered Jack Mountain, this 50-acre natural lake is fed by snow runoff and springs that well up from below the lake's surface. The lake is shallow, with lots of prime habitat for fish and insects. The weed beds are full of nymphs, including Callibaetis, grey drakes, damselflies, dragonflies, Chironomids, and numerous still-water-dwelling caddis. Add in the abundant leech and scud populations, and you can see why the rainbows and brookies grow fat here.

Spring and early summer are the best times to fish Lost Lake. By late summer the lake gets very low (at the highway end) yet has decent water toward the far end. This low-water period is a good time to wade the many shallow areas. Most of the year, however, a float tube or pram is the best way to reach the fish.

Lost Lake is just 28 miles west of Sisters on Highway 20. It is about two miles from Santiam Junction and is easily accessible from Salem, Eugene, and Corvallis, making it a popular destination for Oregon fly fishers.

Lost Lake can be excellent for rainbow and brook trout. Photo by Pete Chadwell.

Types of Fish
Rainbow and brook trout.

Known Hatches
Callibaetis, grey drakes, midges, damselflies, dragonflies, long-horned caddis, traveling sedge, and flying ants. Also important are leeches, scuds, waterboatmen, and snails.

Equipment to Use
Rods: 4 or 5 weight, 8½–10 feet in length.
Reels: Click or disk drag.
Lines: Floating, intermediate, and type-2 full sink.
Leaders: 4X to 6X, 9–15 feet in length; 7½ feet for sinking lines.
Wading & Tubing: Use neoprene waders early in the season, lightweight waders from July through September, and felt-soled boots. Many Lost Lake regulars use a kick boat with small oars.

Flies to Use
Dries: Callibaetis Parachute and Spinner, Adams Parachute, Comparadun, Timberline Emerger, Captive Dun, Suspender Midge, Griffith's Gnat, Para-Midge, Adult Damsel, Black Elk Hair Caddis, Tom Thumb, Goddard Caddis, X Caddis, Ant, Red Tarantula, Float-N-Fool.
Nymphs: Beadhead Leech (black, olive, red, yellow, rust), Woolly Bugger, Scud, Water Boatman, Borger's Snail, Prince, Pheasant Tail, Olive Flashback Hare's Ear, Bloodworm, Carey Special, Damsel, Sparkle Pupa, Soft Hackle Hare's Ear, large Gold-Ribbed Hare's Ears.

When to Fish
At more than 4,500 feet in elevation, on Santiam Pass, Lost Lake can remain frozen and snowbound until May. Fishing is usually good in May after ice-out. June and July are the best months, but don't overlook the rest of the season, especially evenings.

Seasons & Limits
The lake is open all year. Ice coverage dictates when you can fish. Catch and release and barbless flies or lures are the law.

Accommodations & Services
All services are available in Sisters. There is a campground at the lake.

Rating
Jeff's Opinion: Not a blue-ribbon fishery but a great hangout of the locals, a favorite tubing lake, and one worth fishing for some nice trout. A good 6.

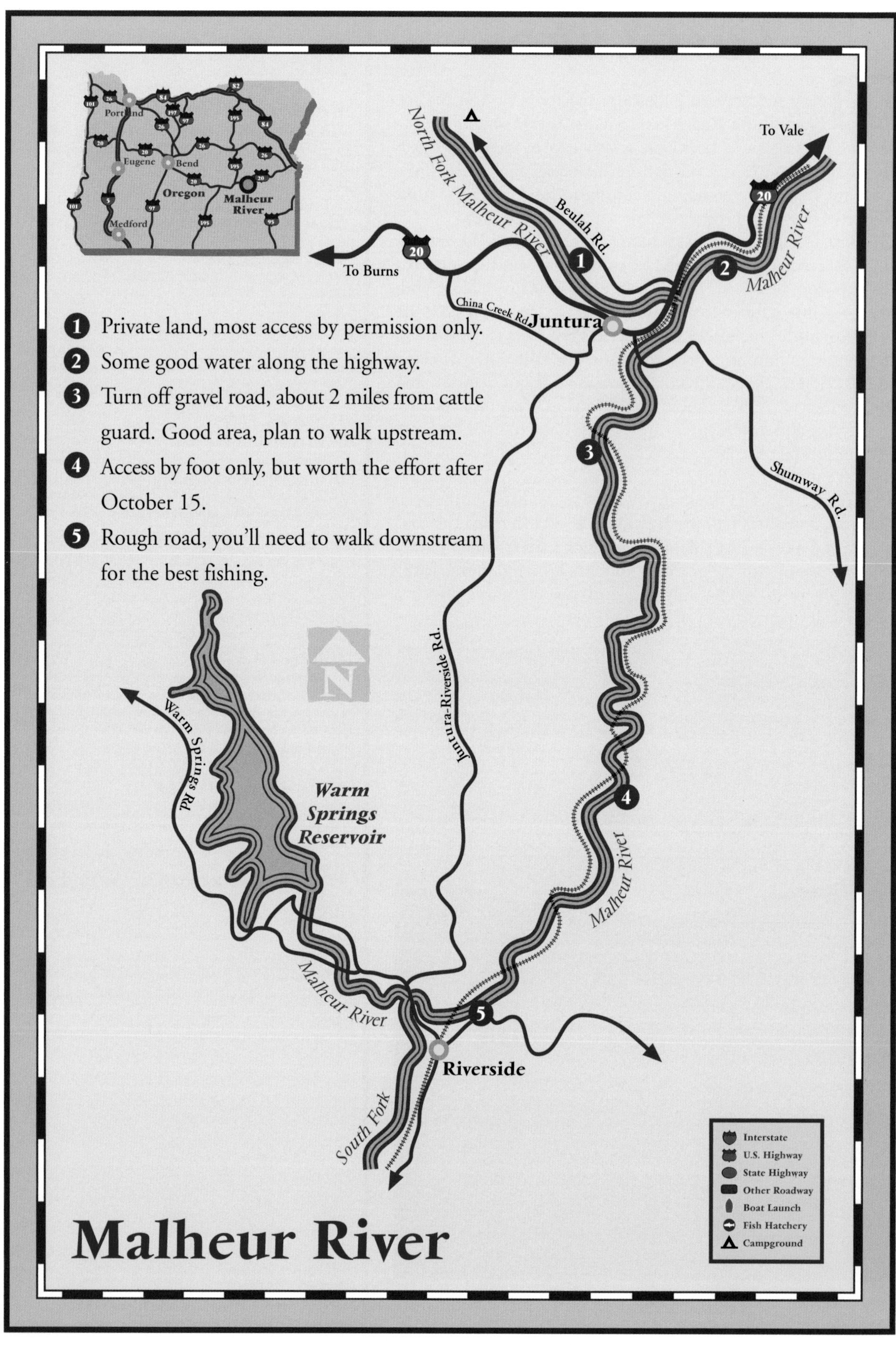
Portland
Eugene
Bend
Oregon
Malheur River
Medford
North Fork Malheur River
Beulah Rd.
To Vale
To Burns
China Creek Rd.
Juntura
Malheur River
Shumway Rd.
1 Private land, most access by permission only.
2 Some good water along the highway.
3 Turn off gravel road, about 2 miles from cattle guard. Good area, plan to walk upstream.
4 Access by foot only, but worth the effort after October 15.
5 Rough road, you'll need to walk downstream for the best fishing.
N
Juntura-Riverside Rd.
Warm Springs Rd.
Warm Springs Reservoir
Malheur River
Riverside
South Fork
Interstate
U.S. Highway
State Highway
Other Roadway
Boat Launch
Fish Hatchery
Campground
Malheur River

Malheur River

The main stem of the Malheur and also its North Fork offer some of the finest fall trout fishing I've ever experienced. I like to fly fish the main river from Riverside to about 10 miles below Juntura. I fish the North Fork above Beulah Reservoir. Beulah can be a good place for large trout if the reservoir hasn't been severely drawn down. Try the east-shore shallows, especially in the fall. You don't have to be very sophisticated on the Malheur either. Attractor-type flies work well, as do large streamer types. You can even fish Hoppers in the heat of July through September.

The fishing in the main river is far and away the best from mid-October (after the irrigation season) until the winter weather makes you seek a warm fire and a good book. You can fish the North Fork nearly any time, but it will require some fairly strenuous walking.

The area of the main Malheur where I fish is about 65 miles east of Burns on Highway 20. As a matter of interest, the headwaters of the Malheur are in the Strawberry Range, and it flows into the Snake River on the Oregon-Idaho border.

Because of high and turbid water conditions, there is little reason for the fly fisher to venture to the main stem of the Malheur during the spring and summer, hence the rating of less than 10. Late fall is another story. I can't think of a place I'd rather be than on the Malheur.

An afternoon on the Malheur River.
Photo by Brian O'Keefe.

Types of Fish
The Malheur is primarily a rainbow trout fishery.

Known Hatches
Mayflies, caddis, and terrestrials.

Equipment to Use
Rods: 3–6 weight, 9–9½ feet in length.
Reels: Palm drag.
Lines: Floating line to match rod weight.
Leaders: 4X to 6X, 9 feet in length.
Wading: Lots of walking is necessary here, so use light wading equipment. Hip boots are fine, or simply wear wading shoes and lightweight pants.

Flies to Use
Dries: Hopper, Royal Wulff, Olive and Rusty Spinners, Comparadun, Renegade, Adams, Elk Hair Caddis.
Nymphs: Hare's Ear, Prince, Pheasant Tail.
Streamers: Woolly Worm, Muddler, Sculpin.

When to Fish
The best-quality fishing on the Malheur is usually after October 15. This is when the river ceases to be an irrigation conduit for the rich farmland of the Treasure Valley.

Seasons & Limits
The Malheur River is open all year; however, regulations and limits are subject to change. There is also private property to consider, so refer to the Oregon Department of Fish & Wildlife regulations and consult a fly shop for current information.

Accommodations & Services
There are limited facilities in the fishable area of the Malheur. Juntura has a motel and restaurant. Be sure you have a full tank of gas when driving in this area.

Rating
Harry's Opinion: I've spent many wonderful fall days on the Malheur with my wife and friends. Mostly we fish, but we also hunt chukar. If you're looking for a place to spend a delightful fall, both fly fishing and bird hunting, take a fling at the Malheur between Riverside and Juntura. The Malheur, in the fall or spring when the water is right, is a 7. During the summer, when it's an irrigation conduit, it's a 1.

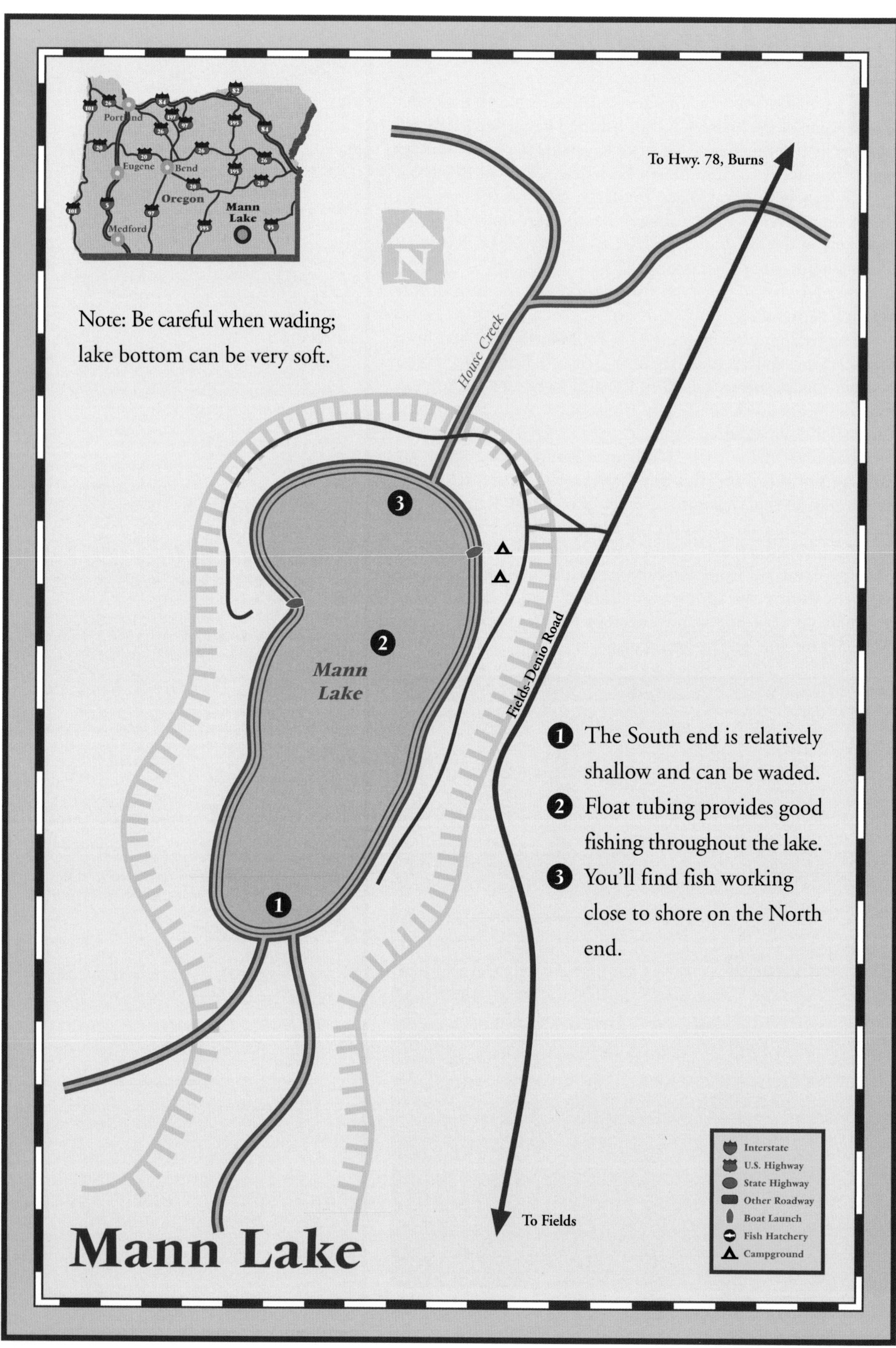
Portland
Eugene
Bend
Oregon
Medford
Mann Lake
To Hwy. 78, Burns
N
Note: Be careful when wading; lake bottom can be very soft.
House Creek
Mann Lake
Fields-Denio Road
1 The South end is relatively shallow and can be waded.
2 Float tubing provides good fishing throughout the lake.
3 You'll find fish working close to shore on the North end.
To Fields
Interstate
U.S. Highway
State Highway
Other Roadway
Boat Launch
Fish Hatchery
Campground
Mann Lake

Mann Lake

Mann Lake is remote. If there is such a thing as a pure desert lake, this is it. With the Steens Mountain Range as a backdrop and the desert floor as a stage, Mann Lake will dazzle you with exceptional desert scenery and good-sized fish. It's roughly 270 acres in size and only 10 to 15 feet deep (may vary with precipitation), but large enough for lots of elbow room.

The alkaline desert water of Mann is perfect for the Lahontan-like cutthroat trout that thrive here. The state of Oregon places fingerlings here every other year, and they quickly grow up to 24 inches in length. (For more about the Lahontan trout, its history and range see the *No Nonsense Guide to Nevada's Pyramid Lake,* by Terry Barron.)

Wading is difficult because of the lake's soft bottom. It is possible to get to the fish by wading, but it's hard work and in some areas you're in muck up to your knees. The best way to fish Mann is from a float tube, the choice of most experienced Mann Lake fly fishers. Boats and canoes are also used.

Mann Lake lies on the east side of the Steens Mountain Range. Take Highway 78 out of Burns and turn south on the Fields-Denio Road (some maps call it Folly Farm Road). This is a good gravel road. From the turnoff on Highway 78 it's about 35 miles to Mann Lake.

Steens Mountain adds beauty to an otherwise desolate environment. Photo by Brian O'Keefe.

Types of Fish

Cutthroat from 12 to 20 inches, with some being a little larger.

Known Hatches

Damselflies.

Equipment to Use

Rods: 4–7 weight depending on the weather, 9–10 feet in length.
Reels: Palm and mechanical drag.
Lines: Floating line to match rod weight.
Leaders: 3X to 5X, 9 feet in length.
Wading: It's best to use a float tube, so bring chest-high waders, boots, and fins. Mann is also a good place for prams, canoes, and other boats.

Flies to Use

You'll have the best results on Mann Lake using nymphs and streamers*:* Zug Bug, Prince, Brassie, Serendipity, Chironomid, Woolly Bugger, Leech, Damsel, and Zonker.

When to Fish

As soon as the ice is off the lake in the spring, things start to happen, usually by late March. This action continues until the water warms in July and August. Good fishing starts again in late September and October. The time of day doesn't seem to make much difference.

Seasons & Limits

Mann Lake is open year-round. Fishing is restricted to barbless flies and lures. All fish under 16 inches must be returned to the lake unharmed. The limit is two fish over 16 inches. As regulations are subject to change, refer to the Oregon Department of Fish & Wildlife regulations or a fly shop for current regulations.

Accommodations & Services

There are no accommodations or services within 50 miles of the lake. The campground on the north end of the lake is unimproved, and no drinking water is available. If you need something, you'll have to travel the 50 miles south to Fields (they have great hamburgers at Fields) or the Princeton/Crane area, or return to Burns. The gravel roads in this area are well maintained but have a reputation as tire eaters. Several years ago I had two blowouts in 35 miles. It took a lot of the fun out of the day. Be sure your gas tank, spare tire, and water containers are full before departing for Mann Lake.

Rating

Harry's Opinion: If you haven't experienced fly fishing a desert lake, try Mann. In the spring and fall, Mann is an exceptional fishery. A word of warning: wind. There are times when the wind prevents fly fishing and forces you to park your car on top of your tent to keep it from blowing into Idaho. A very solid 6.5.

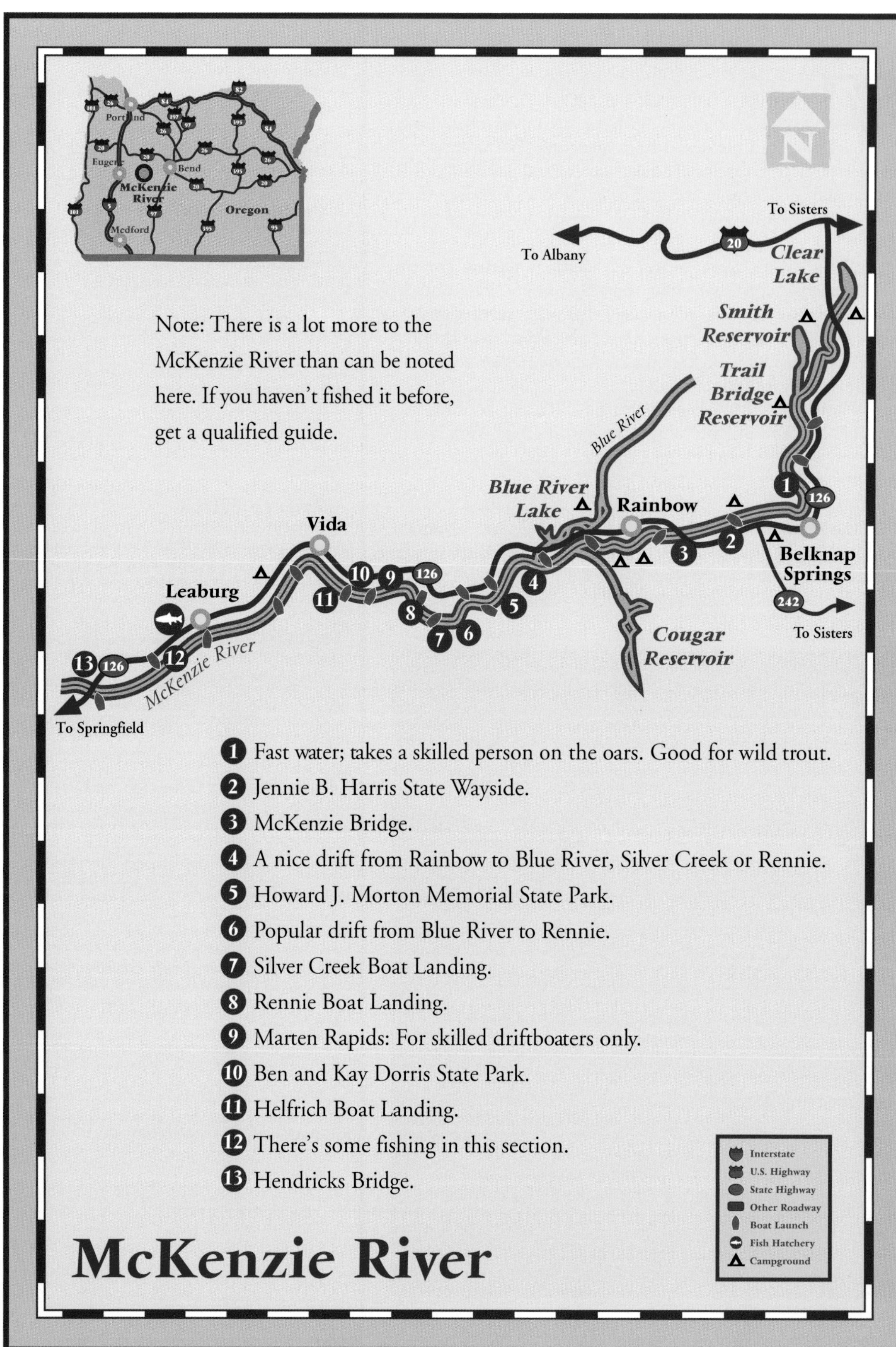
Portland
Eugene
Bend
McKenzie River
Oregon
Medford
N
To Sisters
To Albany
20
Clear Lake
Smith Reservoir
Trail Bridge Reservoir
Blue River
Blue River Lake
Rainbow
126
Belknap Springs
242
To Sisters
Cougar Reservoir
Vida
Leaburg
McKenzie River
To Springfield
Note: There is a lot more to the McKenzie River than can be noted here. If you haven't fished it before, get a qualified guide.
1 Fast water; takes a skilled person on the oars. Good for wild trout.
2 Jennie B. Harris State Wayside.
3 McKenzie Bridge.
4 A nice drift from Rainbow to Blue River, Silver Creek or Rennie.
5 Howard J. Morton Memorial State Park.
6 Popular drift from Blue River to Rennie.
7 Silver Creek Boat Landing.
8 Rennie Boat Landing.
9 Marten Rapids: For skilled driftboaters only.
10 Ben and Kay Dorris State Park.
11 Helfrich Boat Landing.
12 There's some fishing in this section.
13 Hendricks Bridge.
Interstate
U.S. Highway
State Highway
Other Roadway
Boat Launch
Fish Hatchery
Campground
McKenzie River

McKenzie River

The McKenzie is one of the most beautiful rivers in the West. The McKenzie drift boat, a boat type that is now used worldwide, originated on this river. President Herbert Hoover spent much of his fishing life on the McKenzie, and so have a lot of other people. There are numerous good resorts and motels located on or adjacent to the river. A night or two in these comfortable lodgings, coupled with a guided fly fishing drift, is one of the better recreational investments you'll make. The McKenzie has limited access due to private property and a very difficult shoreline to wade. I suggest you retain the services of a qualified McKenzie River guide.

Rainbow trout, steelhead, and salmon call the McKenzie home. Upstream from Blue River is the wild trout section. More than 6,600 rainbows are planted each year from Blue River downstream to Leaburg Lake. More than 2,000 trout are planted in Leaburg Lake, a favorite place to take kids fishing. Some summer steelhead and salmon fishing is available below Leaburg Dam.

For trout anglers, the McKenzie has hatches of caddis, mayflies, some stones and terrestrials. When the season opens in late April, the dry fly activity is just starting, heralded by the March browns (mayflies). Many McKenzie river guides prefer a still, overcast day for dry fly fishing. For salmon and steelhead, the season is generally best in the winter and spring and the fishing is downstream of the dam and the town of Vida.

From central Oregon, travel west of Sisters on Highway 26 about 50 miles and you will come to the best fishing section on the McKenzie. Highway 26 parallels the river from its source at Clear Lake on down to Eugene.

Float fishing on the McKenzie River.
Photo by Brian O'Keefe.

Types of Fish
There are two types of rainbows: stocked and native, plus salmon and steelhead. The native fish are referred to as redsides, and range from 12 to 20 inches. The stocked fish run from 8 to 12 inches. Hatchery fish have the adipose fin clipped. Release all non-fin-clipped trout.

Known Hatches & Baitfish
Caddis, mayflies (March brown), some stones, and terrestrials.

Equipment to Use
Rods: 5–7 weight, 8–9 feet in length.
Reels: Mechanical and palm drag.
Lines: For trout, either a floating or sink tip line will serve you, though you'll probably use your floating line the majority of the time.
Leaders: When fishing dry, 4X to 5X, 9 feet in length. For nymphs, 3X to 4X, 9 feet in length, with a strike indicator.
Wading: There are not many good wading areas; they are isolated, you must search for them, and there is lots of bank vegetation and private property. It's best to drift this stream.

Flies to Use
Dries: Adams, Renegade, Stimulator, Henryville Special, Light Cahill, Flying Ant, Royal Wulff, Humpy, Elk Hair Caddis, Comparadun. I've also seen October Caddis patterns work well.
Nymphs & Streamers: Prince, Hare's Ear, Pheasant Tail, Sparkle Pupa, Black Woolly Bugger.
For Steelhead: Skunk, Green-Butt Skunk, Silver Hilton, Purple Peril.

When to Fish
The heavyweight guides like the river best from late May to early September. You can generally catch fish all day long because there are always some sections of the river in shadow.

Seasons & Limits
The upper river is open from late April to the end of October, and angling is restricted to artificial flies and lures and mostly catch and release for wild trout. Parts of the lower river are open year-round. For exact dates and limits, check the Oregon Department of Fish & Wildlife regulations or ask at a local fly shop.

Accommodations & Services
Stores, restaurants, and gas stations are available from McKenzie Bridge to Walterville. For those not fishing, there's excellent golf nearby at the Tokatee Golf Club.

Rating
Harry's Opinion: For sheer fishing pleasure on one of the West's most notable streams, the McKenzie offers one of life's great rewards. But, as I said, go with a qualified guide. The McKenzie River, with a guide, is a strong 7.

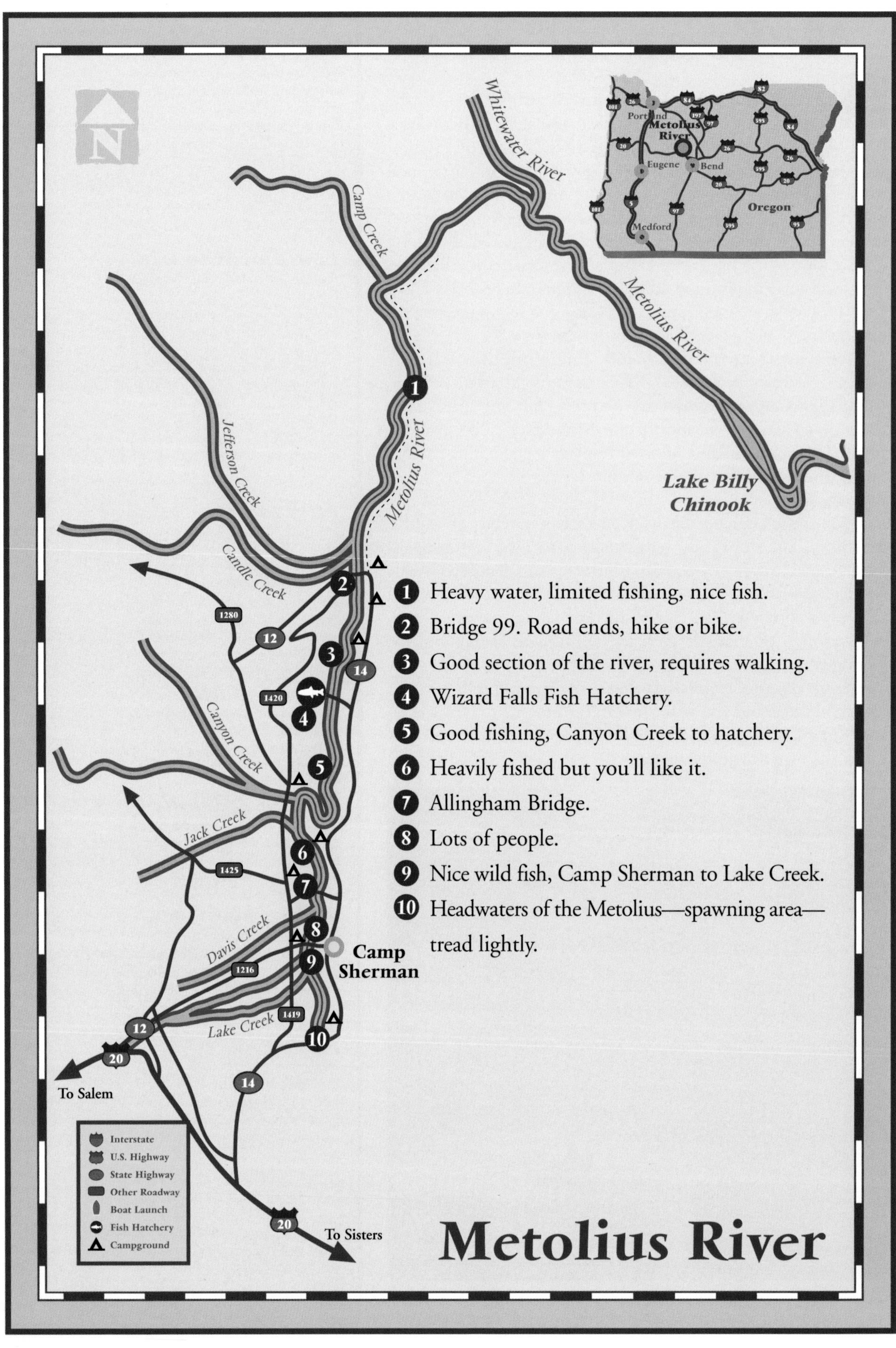

N
Whitewater River
Camp Creek
Metolius River
Jefferson Creek
Candle Creek
Canyon Creek
Jack Creek
Davis Creek
Lake Creek
Lake Billy Chinook
Camp Sherman
To Salem
To Sisters
Portland
Metolius River
Eugene
Bend
Medford
Oregon
1280
12
1420
14
1425
1216
1419
20
1 Heavy water, limited fishing, nice fish.
2 Bridge 99. Road ends, hike or bike.
3 Good section of the river, requires walking.
4 Wizard Falls Fish Hatchery.
5 Good fishing, Canyon Creek to hatchery.
6 Heavily fished but you'll like it.
7 Allingham Bridge.
8 Lots of people.
9 Nice wild fish, Camp Sherman to Lake Creek.
10 Headwaters of the Metolius—spawning area—tread lightly.
Interstate
U.S. Highway
State Highway
Other Roadway
Boat Launch
Fish Hatchery
Campground
Metolius River

Metolius River

The Metolius flows through a beautiful setting of old-growth pine forests with spectacular mountain views. The camping facilities are excellent and help make this a wonderful family recreation area.

In August 1995 the Metolius went to wild fish only and all stocking was halted. This, along with some regulation changes, has been a very positive development. Trout here often don't rise like fish in other rivers do, so it's important to fool them with patterns they perceive to be an easy meal. The Metolius has an assortment of hatches at certain places on the river, daily and throughout the year. Yes, it is complicated. In general, mayflies hatch year-round and caddis hatch from early spring to late fall. The evening caddis emergence is best in summer. From late June through September stonefly hatches on the Metolius are amazing. You should also experiment with transitional or crippled dry fly patterns.

The Metolius is a fine fishing resource. Its crystal clear waters are tricky, and it will take you some time to learn the river's idiosyncrasies, so be realistic with your expectations. A one-fish day is a good day on the Metolius. Catch more than that and you are really on to something. The bull trout fishery here is one of the best in the United States. Consult a local fly shop on how to approach these char. (For an excellent overview of Metolius bull trout and the natural history of the area consult *Seasons of the Metolius* by John Judy.)

I recommend a visit to the headwaters of the Metolius. This site offers one of the most beautiful scenes in the Northwest. The river starts from springs near the base of Black Butte. The view of snow-clad Mt. Jefferson from across the meadow and river is spectacular.

The Metolius is approximately 15 miles northwest of Sisters off Highway 20 on Forest Route 14. Route 14 parallels the river.

A big Metolius River rainbow.
Photo by Brian O'Keefe.

Types of Fish

Predominantly rainbows, with some brown trout and whitefish, running 11 to 18 inches. Bull trout can get to 15 pounds but average three to five pounds. Kokanee (landlocked salmon) run and spawn in the fall.

Known Hatches

Stones, caddis, mayflies, midges, and terrestrials.

Equipment to Use

Rods: 1–7 weight, 6½–9 feet in length.
Reels: Click or disk drag is fine.
Lines: Floating line is best. For bull trout, use a sink tip.
Leaders: 5X to 7X, 12–18 feet in length for dry fishing. For wet or nymph fishing, 9–12 feet in length, with a strike indicator.
Wading: Use chest-high breathable waders and felt-soled boots.

Flies to Use

Dries: Sparkle, Captive, and Knock Down Dun; Comparadun; Thorax Ties and Spinners to match baetis; Pale Morning Dun; Green Drake; Cinygmula; Mahogany Dun; Pale Evening Dun; Flav's; Elk Hair Caddis; CDC; Parachute; Henryville Special; Slow Water and X Caddis; Clark's Stone; Sofa Pillow; Stimulator; Yellow Sally; Olive CDC; Parachute Adams.
Nymphs: Beadhead Pheasant Tail, Prince or Flashback, Hare's Ear, Zug Bug, Golden Stone, October Caddis, Soft Hackle, Brassie.
Streamers: Sculpin, Zonker, White Rabbit Leech.

When to Fish

The river fishes pretty well year-round. Move up- and downstream to find feeding fish. There can be excellent action from November through March. I've never found the Metolius to be an early-morning stream: The best results seem to occur after 9:30 a.m.

Seasons & Limits

Trout fishing is catch and release with barbless hooks only. No weight of any kind is allowed on your line or leader. Use weighted flies for nymphing. Fly fishing only from Bridge 99 upstream to the private property boundary near the walk-in campgrounds. In winter, fly fishing is allowed only below Allingham Bridge. No boats or tubes. Check at a fly shop or consult the Oregon Department of Fish & Wildlife synopsis for areas with special regulations.

Accommodations & Services

You'll find very good lodging, restaurants, and stores at Camp Sherman, Black Butte Ranch, and Sisters.

Rating

Harry & Jeff's Opinion: One of our favorites and a gem by any standards. A challenging river for moderate to expert fly fishing abilities. Learn it, protect it, and enjoy it. The Metolius is a strong 8.

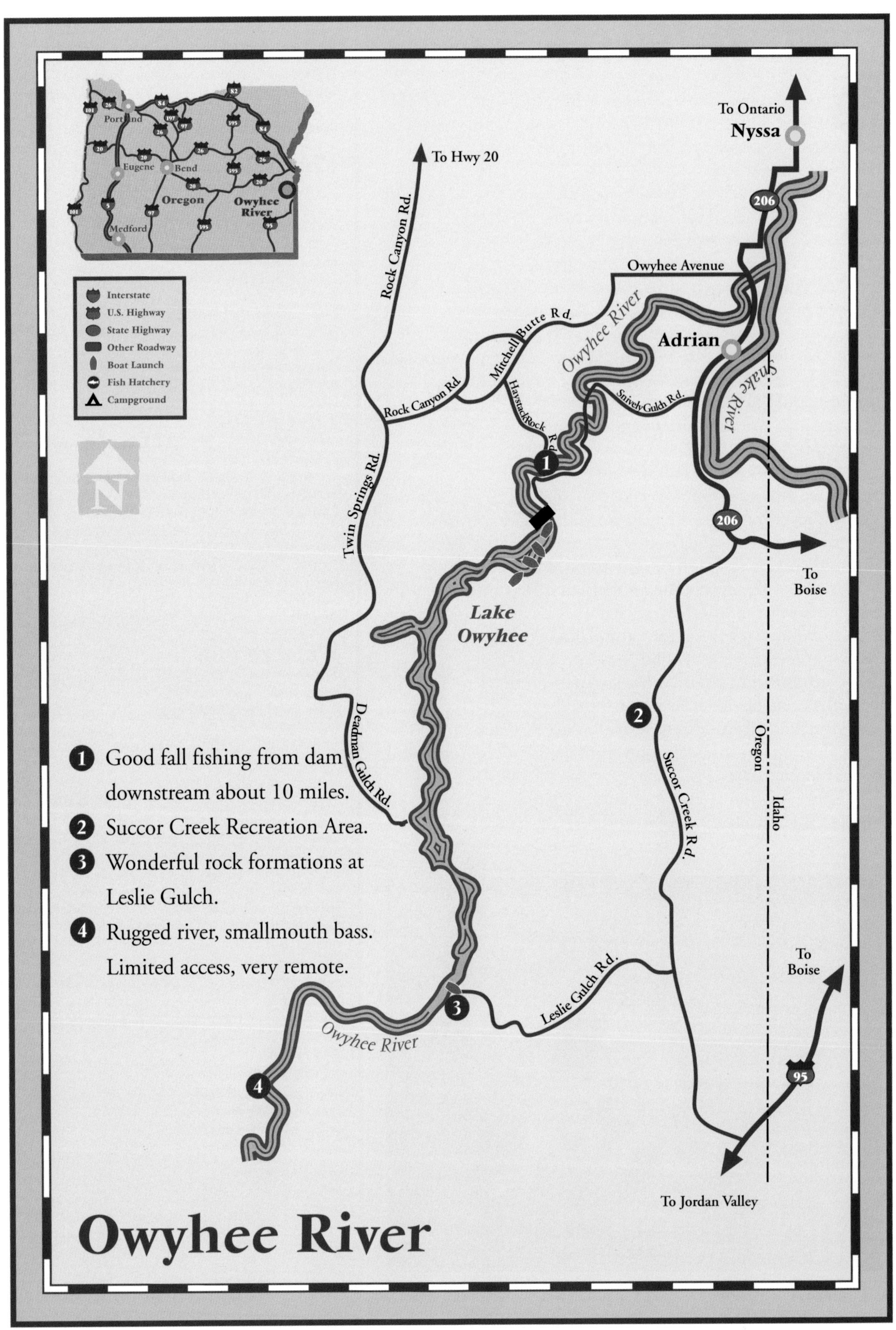
Interstate
U.S. Highway
State Highway
Other Roadway
Boat Launch
Fish Hatchery
Campground
Portland
Eugene
Bend
Medford
Oregon
Owyhee River
To Ontario
Nyssa
To Hwy 20
Rock Canyon Rd.
Owyhee Avenue
Mitchell Butte Rd.
Owyhee River
Adrian
Snake River
Rock Canyon Rd.
Haystack Rock Rd.
Snively Gulch Rd.
Twin Springs Rd.
206
To Boise
Lake Owyhee
Deadman Gulch Rd.
Succor Creek Rd.
Oregon
Idaho
1 Good fall fishing from dam downstream about 10 miles.
2 Succor Creek Recreation Area.
3 Wonderful rock formations at Leslie Gulch.
4 Rugged river, smallmouth bass. Limited access, very remote.
Leslie Gulch Rd.
Owyhee River
To Boise
95
To Jordan Valley
Owyhee River

Owyhee River

The Owyhee, pronounced Oh-wa-hee, is believed to be an early mispronunciation of *Hawaii.* The river runs east from its source in Nevada toward the town of Adrian and then flows into the Snake River. The only part of the Owyhee River I'll address here is that part flowing from Owyhee Dam downstream about 10 miles.

One key to fly fishing here is a stable water flow. Summer is usually fine; fall and winter can be low or too low, depending on how much water is needed behind the dam. The river can also freeze over in winter. Call the Oregon Department of Fish & Wildlife office in Ontario, Oregon, for flows and current information: 541-889-6975. The Oregon Department of Fish & Wildlife stocks this river every other year with brown trout. Every year they plant some 40,000 rainbows. It is not known if trout naturally reproduce in the Owyhee.

The Owyhee is a fairly good-sized river, and long casts are sometimes needed. The river has all types of fly water too, including riffles, runs, pools, pockets, and runs full of boulders. My experience is that small patterns produce the best results.

The geological formations along this river section are fantastic. The rock formations and colors are stunning, to say the least. Even if you don't fish, the trip up the Owyhee River to the dam and Lake Owyhee is worth your time. In the fall, you can combine fishing with chukar hunting. You'll find plenty of both. The river is always off-color (milky) but don't let that bother you. It's very fishable.

The cliffs on the Owyhee River dwarf this fly fisher. Photo by Brian O'Keefe.

Types of Fish

Rainbows from 7 to 15 inches, and good brown trout up to 20 inches.

Known Hatches

There are hatches of midges, caddis, and mayflies during the spring, summer, and fall.

Equipment to Use

Rods: 4–7 weight, 8–9 feet in length.
Reels: Palm drag is fine.
Lines: Floating line to match rod weight.
Leaders: 4X and 5X, 9 feet in length.
Wading: Use waist-high or chest-high breathable waders and felt-soled wading shoes. Always carry a wading staff for probing the bottom in the off-colored water. Wade with care.

Flies to Use

Dries: Adams; Captive Dun; Elk Hair Caddis; Comparadun; Pale Morning Dun; Rusty, Olive, and Black Spinners; Blue-Winged Olive; Renegade (#16 and #18), X Caddis; Slow Water Caddis.
Nymphs: Hare's Ear, Midge Pupa, Beadhead Pheasant Tail, Scud, Sparkle Pupa, Beadhead Serendipity, Prince and Chironomid Pupa.
Streamers: Zonker, Woolly Bugger, Marabou Muddler.

When to Fish

I like the fall, from mid-September through October. The fish are active on the surface and are eager to attack almost anything that is properly presented. Fishing is good all day. It doesn't appear that one time is any better than another, but I favor afternoon and evening fishing.

Seasons & Limits

The Owyhee below the dam is open year-round and has been catch and release only for browns. This may change, so check at a fly shop or consult the current Oregon Department of Fish & Wildlife regulations for seasons and limits.

Accommodations & Services

There are a lot of good campsites along the river. Most are unimproved. Overnight accommodations, restaurants, gas, and groceries can be found in Adrian, Nyssa, and the resort on Lake Owyhee.

Rating

Harry's Opinion: The Owyhee River is a great place to spend time in the fall. The fishing can be very good. It's picturesque and there is plenty of sightseeing in the area. While you are there, you should drive through the Succor Creek State Recreation Area and Leslie Gulch. These areas have exceptionally beautiful rock formations, canyons, and other geologic features. The Owyhee rates a soft 5, but devoted Owyhee fly fishers won't agree with this low rating.

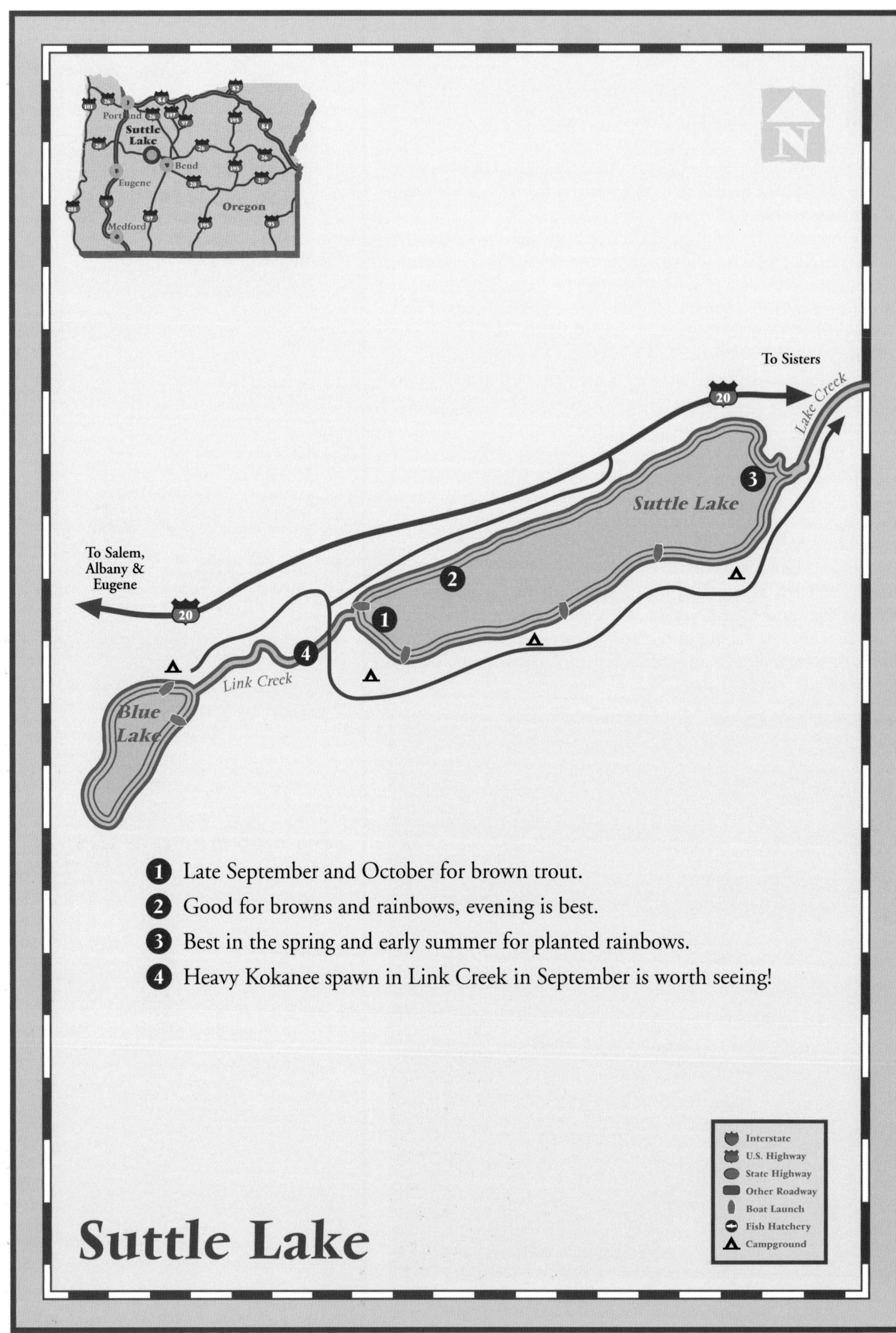
Portland
Suttle Lake
Bend
Eugene
Oregon
Medford
N
To Sisters
Lake Creek
20
Suttle Lake
3
To Salem,
Albany &
Eugene
2
1
4
Link Creek
Blue Lake
❶ Late September and October for brown trout.
❷ Good for browns and rainbows, evening is best.
❸ Best in the spring and early summer for planted rainbows.
❹ Heavy Kokanee spawn in Link Creek in September is worth seeing!
Suttle Lake
Interstate
U.S. Highway
State Highway
Other Roadway
Boat Launch
Fish Hatchery
Campground

Suttle Lake

Suttle Lake is surrounded by pine forest and there are some excellent views of the nearby Cascade Mountains. As of this writing, a small resort on the lake's east shore rents boats; has a dock, store, and restaurant; and offers a base for non-angling family members. There are plans to expand the resort, and the expansion may be complete by the time you read this.

When a lake is this easy to get to, you wouldn't expect it to have a good population of large brown trout. Nonetheless, Suttle has them and they can be taken with flies. You'll also find rainbow trout and a strong population of kokanee (landlocked salmon). Browns run from one to five pounds, with a few being bigger. Rainbows are planted and average from 8 to 12 inches. Kokanee are in the 9- to 14-inch range. As you would expect, fly patterns will change depending on the time of year you're fishing Suttle. Ask around or at a local fly shop.

There are only a few good places to wade, most notably near the boat ramp and Link Creek. You can ride a mountain bike around the lake's trail to scout for fish. A float tube is a good way to cover a lot of area with a fly rod. Most people fish Suttle Lake from a boat.

Suttle Lake is one of the better family lakes in the region, with excellent campgrounds and boat launching ramps. A lot of recreational activities are available around the lake, including horseback riding, hiking, and water skiing to name a few.

This large lake is about 15 miles west of Sisters on the south side of Highway 20.

Scenic Suttle Lake near Sisters, Oregon.
Photo by David Banks.

Types of Fish

Wild brown trout, hatchery rainbows, and kokanee salmon.

Known Hatches

Mayflies and midges.

Equipment to Use

Rods: 5–7 weight, 8–9½ feet in length.
Reels: Mechanical and palm drag.
Lines: Floating and sink tip for flexibility.
Leaders: 3X to 5X, 9 feet in length.
Wading: Chest-high, neoprene or breathable waders and felt-soled wading boots. Wading is limited so float tubing or boating is a good Suttle fly fishing method. You'll need the preceding wading equipment for tubing, along with a pair of fins.

Flies to Use

Dries: Renegade, Adams, Royal Wulff, Comparadun.
Nymphs & Streamers: Hare's Ear, Prince, Carey Special, Zonker, Muddler, Woolly Bugger.

When to Fish

You'll find the best fishing in May and June and again in late September and October. For browns, fishing is best late in the year, with late afternoon and evening being most productive. Generally, there aren't any water skiers during these time periods.

Seasons & Limits

Suttle is open all year; most fly fishing is from late April to the end of October. Limits range from five trout per day to 20 kokanee per day and are subject to change. Consult a fly shop or the Oregon Department of Fish & Wildlife regulations for exact dates and bag limits.

Accommodations & Services

There are campgrounds on the south side and west end of the lake. A store, restaurant, and small dock on the east end of the lake are near a beach and group picnic shelter. This resort also rents small cabins and boats (541-595-6662). There are accommodations, restaurants, gas, and groceries in Sisters, Camp Sherman, and Black Butte Ranch.

Rating

Harry's Opinion
If you're looking for an easy-to-access lake with better than average fishing, Suttle is a good choice. It may be the most underrated lake in central Oregon. For overall fishing, Suttle is a 6.5. For fly fishing it's a soft 5.

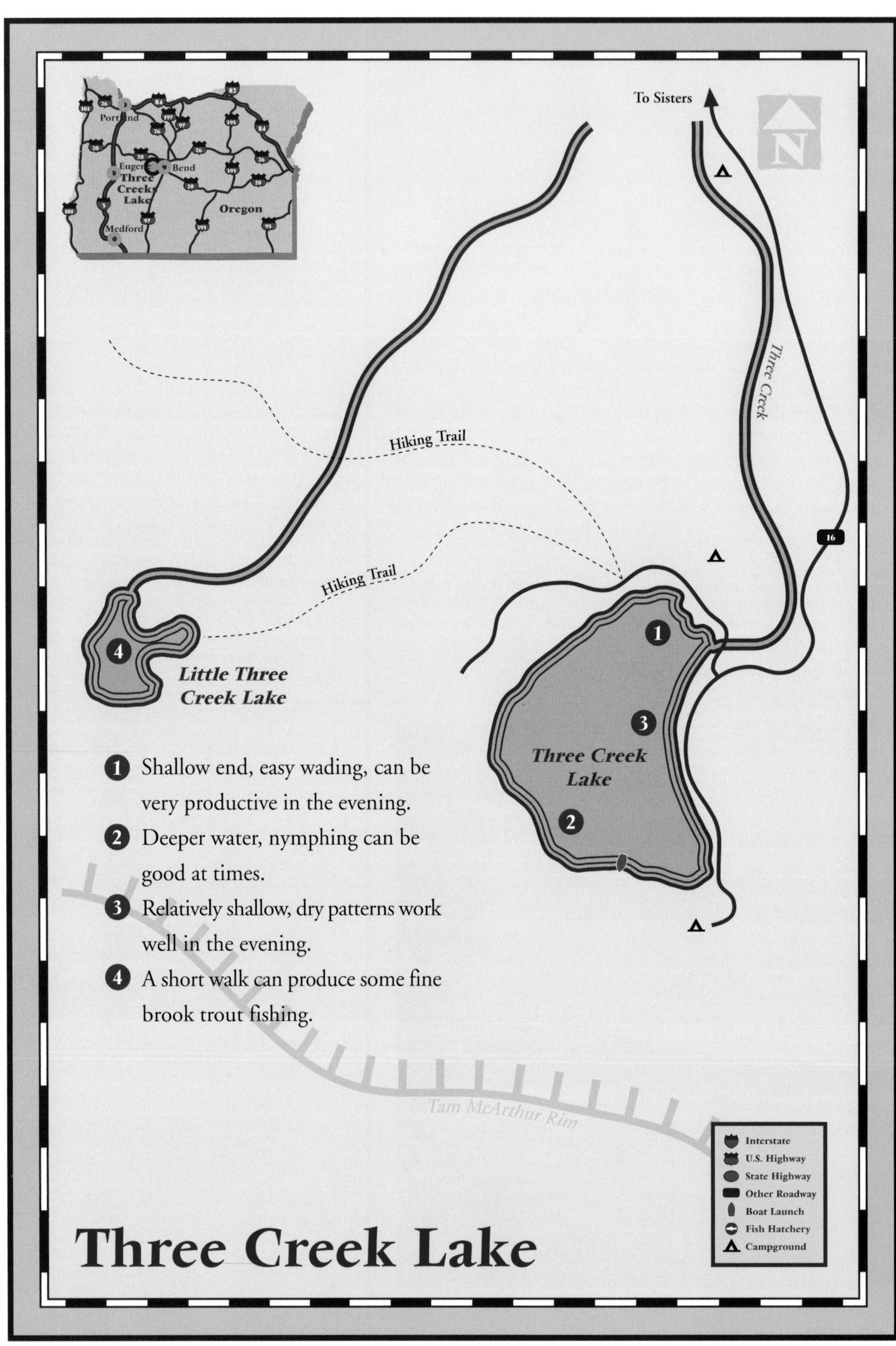

1. Shallow end, easy wading, can be very productive in the evening.
2. Deeper water, nymphing can be good at times.
3. Relatively shallow, dry patterns work well in the evening.
4. A short walk can produce some fine brook trout fishing.

Three Creek Lake

Three Creek Lake

Probably the majority of the traffic going the 18 miles from Sisters to Three Creek Lake is headed for a hike into the scenic Three Sisters Wilderness. There aren't many people headed up there packing fly rods. Just going up to Three Creek Lake is well worth the trip.

South of Sisters, at the base of Broken Top and the Three Sisters Mountains, lie 30-acre Three Creek and 14-acre Little Three Creek Lakes. The bigger lake and its smaller cousin are in a beautiful high Cascade alpine setting at approximately 6,500 feet. Here is a fishing trip that's worth the ride for the scenic value alone. Besides the scenery, odds are in your favor that you'll catch some fish.

Float tubing is a good way to fish the lakes. Cast dry flies if you see a hatch, otherwise sink nymphs and retrieve slowly. If you prefer a boat, or if you have small children, boating works quite well too, but you must row or paddle. Motors are not allowed on either lake. Float tube enthusiasts should note that to get to Little Three Creek Lake from the bigger lake requires about a mile hike from the Driftwood Campground or a 40-minute hike in from the meadow trailhead.

The easiest way to get to the lakes is from downtown Sisters. Take Elm Street, which becomes Forest Road 16, south to the lakes. This road is closed in winter about 15 miles outside of town. Fishing the lakes usually starts in late May depending on snowpack. Carry mosquito repellant.

Looking North across Three Creek Lake from Tam McArthur Rim. Photo by David Banks.

Types of Fish

Three Creek Lake has both rainbow and brook trout ranging from 8 to 15 inches. Little Three Creek Lake has a good population of self-propagating brook trout that grow to about 14 inches. The little lake also has some stocked rainbows in the 12-inch range and a few larger rainbow that manage to hold over from winter to winter.

Known Hatches

Mayflies, damselflies, and midges.

Equipment to Use

Rods: 3-7 weight, 9–10 feet in length.
Reels: Palm drag is adequate.
Lines: Floating line to match rod weight. Some fly fishers like to use a sink tip line, though I haven't found it necessary.
Leaders: 4X and 5X, 9 feet in length.
Wading: There are parts of the lake you can wade. You'll need chest-high waders and wading boots. Float tubes are a good idea.

Flies to Use

Dries: Adams, Renegade, Elk Hair Caddis, Comparadun, Ant, Royal Wulff.
Nymphs: Hare's Ear, Polly Casual Dress, Pheasant Tail, Damsel, Chironomid.

When to Fish

July, August, September, and October are regarded as the best months. The evening hours have the best fly fishing.

Seasons & Limits

The season opens in late April and closes at the end of October. For limits and exact dates, refer to local fly shops or the Oregon Department of Fish & Wildlife regulations.

Accommodations & Services

There are two very nice campgrounds and a seasonal store with boat rentals and a small dock at Three Creek Lake. All other services are available in Sisters. Little Three Creek Lake is a hike-in or pack-in lake. There are no official campgrounds or other services there.

Rating

Harry & Jeff's Opinion: These lakes are fun to fish, especially with a float tube. Three Creek and Little Three Creek rate a soft 6.

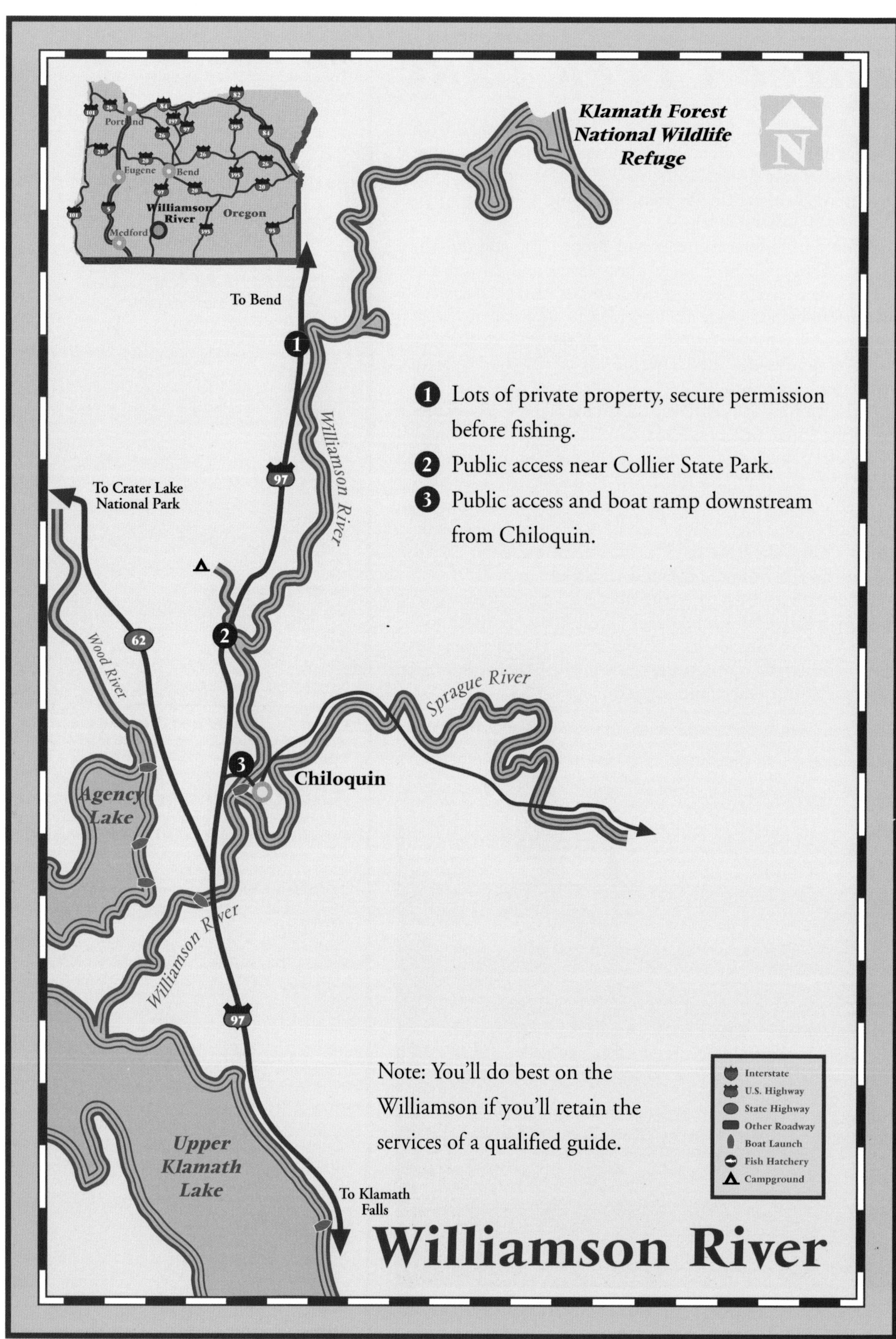
Klamath Forest
National Wildlife
Refuge
N
Portland
Eugene
Bend
Williamson
River
Oregon
Medford
To Bend
❶ Lots of private property, secure permission before fishing.
❷ Public access near Collier State Park.
❸ Public access and boat ramp downstream from Chiloquin.
Williamson River
97
To Crater Lake
National Park
62
Wood River
Sprague River
Chiloquin
Agency
Lake
Williamson River
97
Upper
Klamath
Lake
Note: You'll do best on the Williamson if you'll retain the services of a qualified guide.
Interstate
U.S. Highway
State Highway
Other Roadway
Boat Launch
Fish Hatchery
Campground
To Klamath
Falls
Williamson River

Williamson River

A conversation I had one day with Polly Rosborough, the late and revered fly-tyer, sportsman, and pioneer of the Klamath County Fly Casters, told me a lot about this river in a few words. He said the Williamson is the best "big-fish" water in the country, and I think he was right. The Williamson was one of the first rivers in Oregon to be managed for wild trout.

Fish the Williamson with large flies. Cast a little upstream, let the fly sink and swing, and strip it back. In the summer, fish dries on the surface when the caddis and mayflies hatch. Many people fish the October caddis hatch in the fall. Look for heavy mayfly and caddis hatches in June and July.

The big three-year and older rainbows are not easy to catch. On any given day, however, you'll see more fish in the 5- to 10-pound range splashing around on the surface than you can reasonably imagine. If you want a chance to take big trout, hire a guide and head for the Williamson. If you aren't taking a guide, the Williamson can be tough to learn, especially without a boat. The accompanying map will help.

The Lower Williamson River, the primary fly fishing section, is 25 miles north of Klamath Falls. Highway 97 crosses it near the town of Chiloquin, where the Sprague River enters the Williamson. It's a big, winding river that runs through lots of private, national forest, and cattle land.

A peaceful evening on the glassy Williamson River. Photo by Brian O'Keefe.

Types of Fish
Large rainbow trout and protected Lost River suckers.

Known Hatches
Caddis, October caddis, and mayflies.

Equipment to Use
Rods: 4–7 weight, 8½–9½ feet in length.
Reels: Mechanical and palm drag.
Lines: Floating and sink tip to match rod weight. Some guides like intermediate sink lines.
Leaders: For dries, 4X to 6X, 9–15 feet in length. For nymphs and streamers, 3X and 4X, 9–15 feet in length.
Wading: Use breathable waders, felt-soled boots, and a wading staff.

Flies to Use
Dries: Hexagenia, Elk Hair Caddis, Comparadun, Adams, Humpy, Irresistible, Pale Morning Dun, X Caddis, Trico, Blue-Winged Olive, Black Drake, Grasshopper and other terrestrials.
Nymphs & Streamers: Pheasant Tail, Hare's Ear, Marabou Leech, Matuka, Woolly Bugger, Muddler Minnow, Zonker.

When to Fish
June through October, when the big fish move in from Upper Klamath Lake, is best. A guide suggests that the time of day isn't as important as putting the fly in the right place.

Seasons & Limits
Late May through October. There are varying regulations on the Williamson, I suggest checking the Oregon Department of Fish & Wildlife regulations or asking at a fly shop before fishing.

Accommodations & Services
Good camping facilities are available at Spring Creek and Williamson River. You can find a motel, restaurants, and a service station near Chiloquin and an RV park off Highway 97. Everything else is available in Klamath Falls.

Rating
Harry's Opinion: If you haven't fished for the Williamson's big trout before, you'll save a lot of learning time and effort by hiring a qualified guide. The Williamson rates an 8 for big fish opportunity.

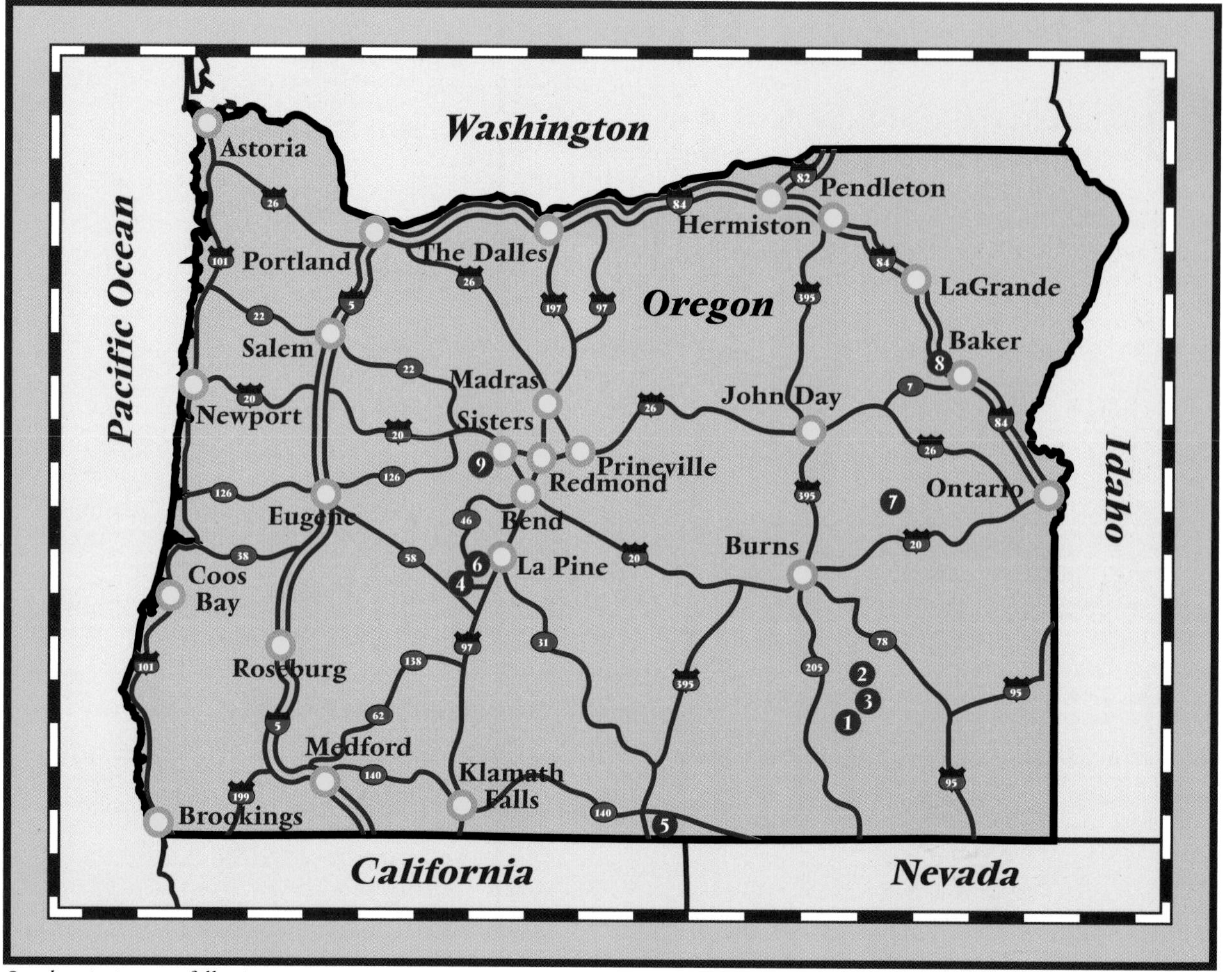

See descriptions on following page.

Other Rivers & Creeks

Here's about all the information you'll need to fly fish these other rivers and streams. Check with one of the fly shops listed in the appendix to get additional details about tackle, hatches, and current conditions.

Types of Fish
Rainbow, brown, brook, and bull trout.

Known Hatches
Mayflies, damselflies, caddis, and midges.

Equipment to Use
Rods: 4–6 weight, 6–9 feet in length.
Reels: Standard trout reels are fine.
Lines: Floating, intermediate sink to type-4.
Leaders: 3X to 4X, 6–12 feet in length.
Wading: Most waters are wadable with hip boots or chest-high waders.

Flies to Use
Dries: Midge, Callibaetis, Elk Hair Caddis, Adams, Humpy, PMD, Blue-Winged Olive, Renegade, Royal Wulff.
Nymphs: Scud, Midge Pupa, Hare's Ear, Pheasant Tail, Bird's Nest, Prince, Zug Bug, Brassie, Golden Stone.
Streamers: Woolly Bugger, Zonker, Matuka, Leech, Muddler.

When to Fish
Consult a fly shop or the Oregon Department of Fish & Wildlife synopsis for the best times to fly fish.

Accommodations & Services
Some, variable, or none! Ask.

Rating
When conditions are good, all are 5 or better.

1. Little Blitzen

The Little Blitzen, a tributary of the Donner und Blitzen, flows into the Blitzen about three miles downstream from Blitzen Crossing. Blitzen Crossing is located on the Steens Mountain Loop Road. The Little Blitzen can be accessed through the Clemens Ranch, which has been deeded to the Bureau of Land Management. For specific information, consult BLM personnel at their office on Highway 20 just west of Hines. The Little Blitzen is fly fishing and catch and release only.

2. Big Indian and Little Indian Creeks

These two creeks are on the west side of the Steens Mountain and can be accessed off the Steens Mountain Loop Road. These small creeks hold good populations of native rainbows. They can't stand much pressure, so please practice catch and release when you fish them. Plan on doing lots of walking. The terrain along these creeks will amaze you. It's really remarkable.

3. Other Steens Mountain Streams

You'll find numerous small creeks cascading down the Steens. Creeks like the Kiger, McCoy, Ankle, Wild Horse, and Skull all hold wild fish. To access some of these, you must cross private land, which can pose a problem. Some may be closed too, so contact the Bureau of Land Management office (on Highway 20 west of Hines) or ODFW for guidance.

4. Crescent Creek

It's hardly a household word in central Oregon, but the Crescent is a nice little fly fishing water. The creek has plenty of access and good populations of brown and rainbow trout. Fly shops in Bend or the Oregon Department of Fish & Wildlife office should be able to assist you with information on Crescent Creek. It can be accessed off Highway 58 west of Highway 97.

5. Deep Creek

Deep Creek is located southeast of Lakeview and more or less parallels Highway 140. This is a good fly fishing stream with stocked and wild fish. Check with the Oregon Department of Fish & Wildlife regional office in Hines for current conditions.

6. Little Deschutes River

This meandering stream crosses Highway 58 east of where Crescent Creek crosses the highway. It has some good-sized brown trout and rainbows and is fairly easy to wade. If you are in a mood for exploring new trout water, you just might give the Little Deschutes a try.

7. North Fork of the Malheur River

The section above Beulah Reservoir, accessible only by foot, can provide some exceptional rainbow fishing. Study a good topographical map and select a likely spot. It's my guess you'll be glad you gave the North Fork a try.

8. Powder River

The Powder is northwest of Baker and is accessed off Highway 30. The best fishing is in the tailwaters of Mason and Thief Valley dams. Rainbows run from 9 to 14 inches with an occasional fish reaching 18 inches.

9. Squaw Creek

If you're in the Sisters area and just want to poke around with a light fly rod, try Squaw Creek. This little creek comes into town from the Cascades and eventually empties into the Deschutes River above Lake Billy Chinook. Most of the fish are wild rainbows. Ten inches is as big as you'll get. Occasionally a big one escapes a farm pond and gets into the creek. Fish with dries like a Madam X, Renegade, or Royal Wulff. Also throw in some Comparaduns, Elk Hair Caddis, and a Griffith's Gnat. For nymphs, use a Brassie, Beadhead Pheasant Tail, Soft Hackle, or Hare's Ear in small sizes. In the summer, forget waders and hop along the rocks. The rest of the year, consider hip waders. Because these fish are wild, we strongly encourage catch and release.

The Little Blitzen River gives up a small and fiesty trout. Photo by Brian O'Keefe.

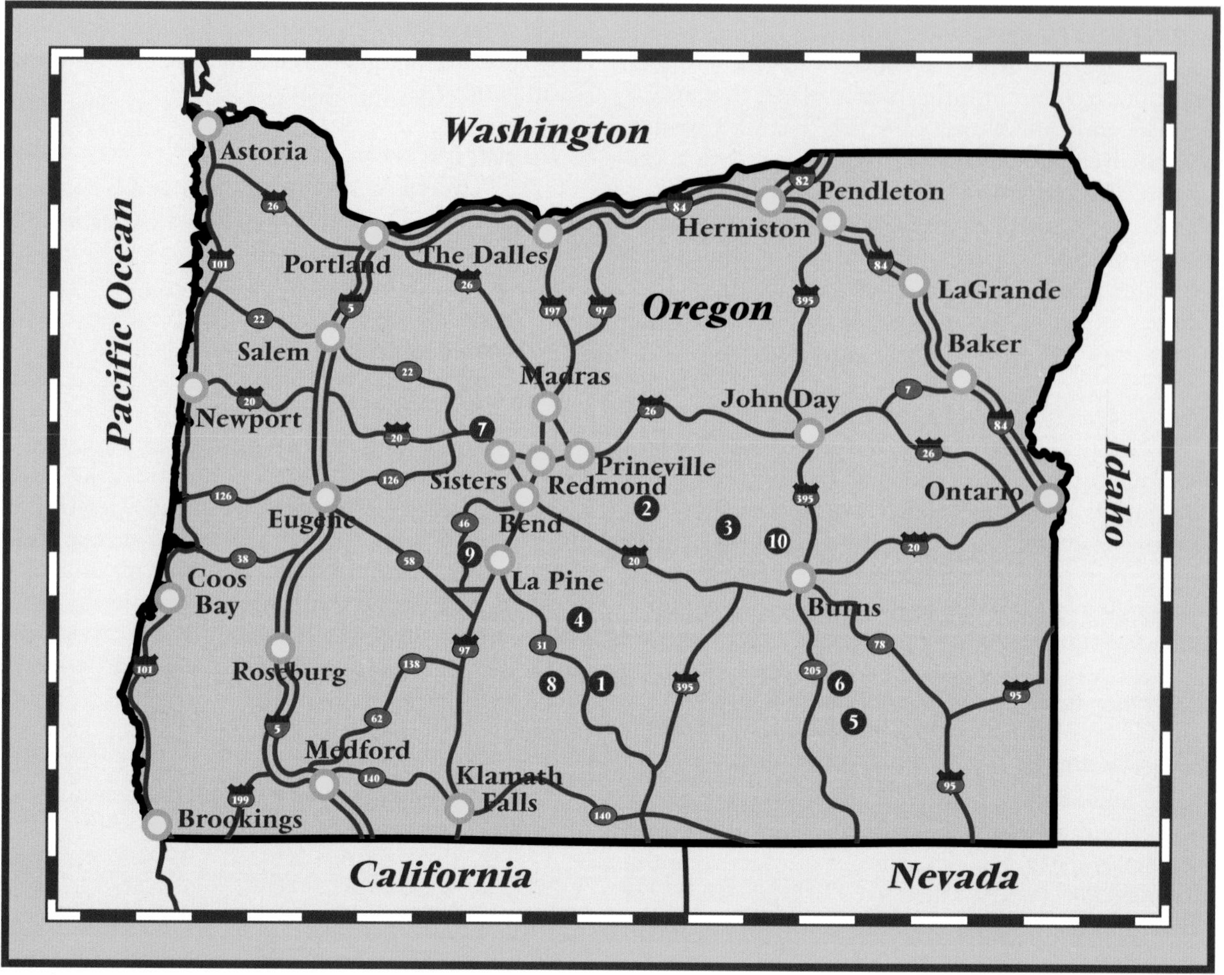

See descriptions on following page.

Other Still Waters

Here's about all the information you'll need to fly fish these other still waters. Check with one of the fly shops listed in the appendix to get additional details about tackle, hatches, and current conditions.

Types of Fish

Rainbow, brown, and brook trout; bass; and bluegill.

Known Hatches

Mayflies, damselflies, caddis, and midges.

Equipment to Use

Rods: 4–7 weight, 6–9½ feet in length.
Reels: Standard trout reels are fine.
Lines: Floating, full sink intermediate to type-4.
Leaders: 3X to 6X, 6–15 feet in length.
Wading: Most waters have wadable shorelines. Take a float tube if you prefer.

Flies to Use

Dries: Damsel, Midge, Callibaetis, Elk Hair Caddis, Timberline Emerger, Griffith's Gnat, Comparadun, Light Cahill.
Nymphs: Scud, Damsel, Dragonfly, Midge, Snail, Gold Ribbed Hare's Ear, Pheasant Tail, Bird's Nest, Prince, Zug Bug, Tied-Down Caddis, Water Boatman.
Streamers: Woolly Bugger, Zonker, Matuka, Leech.

When to Fish

Consult a fly shop or the Oregon Department of Fish & Wildlife synopsis for the best times to fish.

Accommodations & Services

Some, variable, or none! Ask.

Rating

When conditions are good, all are 5 or better.

1. Ana Reservoir

As the source of the Ana River, this small reservoir is ice free most of the year. It's fed by springs with water temperatures of around 56 degrees F. I've had some good days fly fishing here during January and February. The reservoir is stocked with rainbow trout and has a population of hybrid bass. It's not a bad place to go to shrug off the winter fishing blahs.

2. Antelope Flat Reservoir

A fair-sized reservoir of about 170 acres when full. The reservoir is southeast of Prineville. Take the road from Prineville to Paulina (Paulina Highway) and turn south on Forest Road 17, some eight miles east of Post. It's roughly 11 miles to the reservoir. There are campgrounds and a boat launch.

3. Delintment Lake

Delintment is about 50 acres and lies northwest of Burns. For the best access, check with the Bureau of Land Management, Oregon Department of Fish & Wildlife, or at B&B Sporting Goods. All are located in the Burns/Hines area on Highway 20. Rainbows are of good size and it's not unusual to get a fish in the three-pound class. Most fish are 9 to 14 inches. There's a good campground at the lake.

4. Duncan Reservoir

This desert reservoir is near Silver Lake, east of the town of Silver Lake about 50 miles southeast of La Pine on Highway 31. It's had its ups and downs. One day I got a call from Cal Jordan (now deceased) about meeting him to fish Duncan Reservoir. He'd just had the best fly fishing he'd ever experienced in Oregon that day at Duncan. We went the next day, and between us, we didn't have a strike. As I said, Duncan is a good fly fishery, but it has its ups and downs.

5. Fish Lake

The lake is located on Steens Mountain and has plenty of spunky rainbows. Fly fishing can be good from the time you can access the lake (generally late June) until late October. If you go in July, load your rig with mosquito repellant. The fall can be beautiful, and you may have the lake nearly to yourself. Take Steens Mountain Loop from Frenchglen (on Highway 205) to reach the lake. Frenchglen has all services.

6. Krumbo Reservoir

When you're in the vicinity of Frenchglen, you might want to check Krumbo Reservoir. It has a mixed bag of fish (rainbow, bass, etc.), but the rainbows get to be fairly good sized. It has a surface area of about 150 acres. You can reach Krumbo by going south from Burns on Highway 205 toward Frenchglen. It will be on your left about 20 miles from the Malheur Refuge headquarters turnoff. A dirt road leads to the reservoir. It's about four miles from Highway 205 to the reservoir. There is food, gas, lodging, and camping in and near Frenchglen.

7. Round, Square, and Long lakes

These lakes, near Santiam Pass and Sisters, can be accessed by going to Round Lake on Forest Road 1210. You'll have to walk to Square and Long Lakes. You'll find rainbow, cutthroat, and brook trout in these lakes. The fish are not large but can be fun. If you want to take the family on a nice outing or hike, this is a good choice. There is a primitive campground at Round Lake.

8. Thompson Reservoir

Like Chickahominy, Thompson was hit hard by drought but has come back. This is one of the better "other" reservoirs for fly fishing. The rainbows here grow rapidly and fish in the 20-inch range are common. It's best to fish from a boat. Try the fingerlike bays. There are good campgrounds and boat launching facilities. Thompson is about 15 miles south of the community of Silver Lake. Take Highway 31 from La Pine and turn south on Route 27 (Silver Creek Marsh Road).

9. Wickiup Reservoir

This is a large reservoir that has a good population of brown trout. Some are truly giants. Most people think of Wickiup as a hardware fishery, but if you take the time to learn the reservoir, Wickiup can produce excellent results. Get to Wickiup from Sunriver off Route 42 (S. Century Drive).

10. Yellowjacket Lake

A small lake about 40 miles northwest of Burns, Yellowjacket has some nice fish and is stocked annually. It can be fished from the shore, but a float tube is a good idea. There's a good campground at the lake. From Highway 397 south of Burns, turn north on Route 47 to Route 37 east. There is a campground and boat ramp at the lake.

A beautiful brook trout from one of central Oregon's still waters. Photo by David Banks.

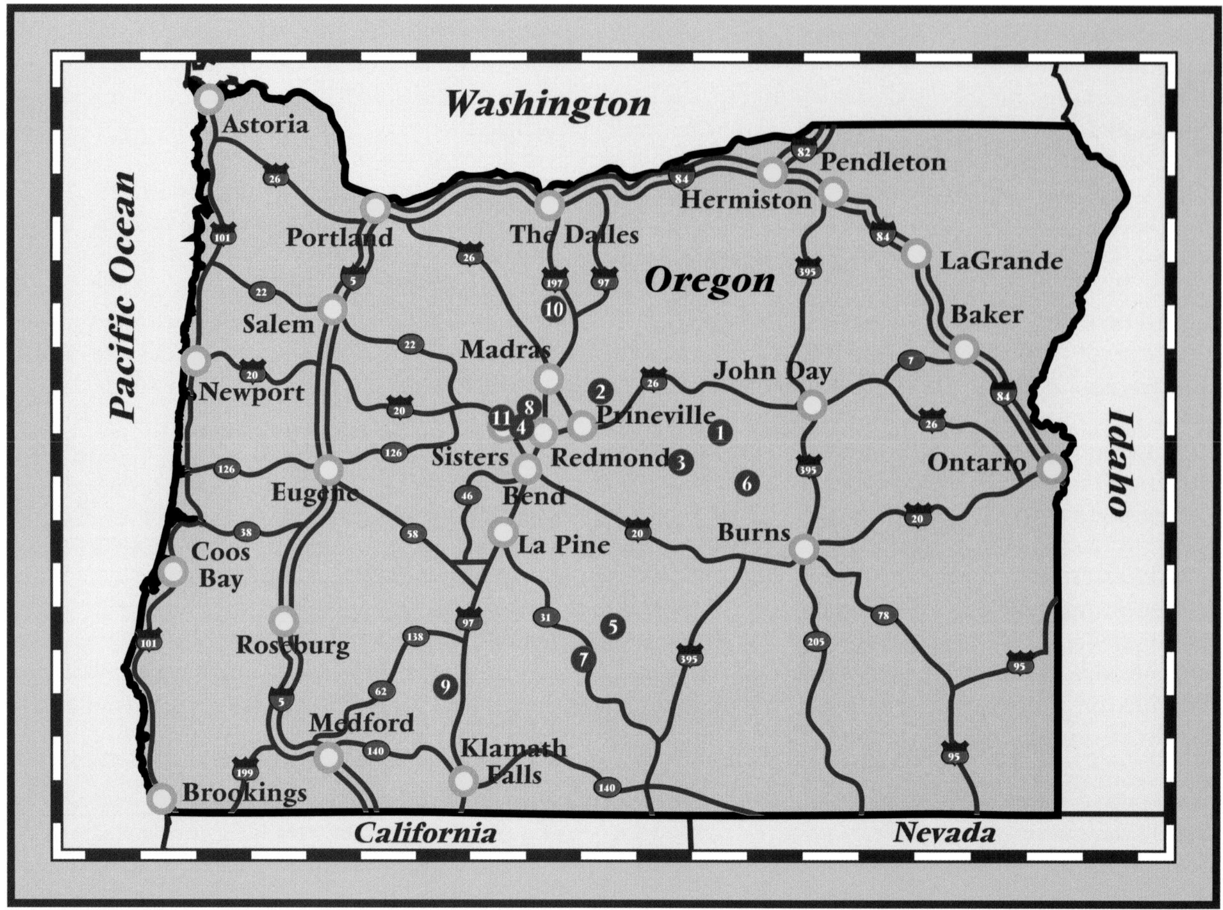

See descriptions on following page.

Private Waters

Central and southeastern Oregon has excellent private alternatives to public fly fishing waters. Pay fly fishing is often the only way to achieve seclusion and reliable fly fishing. But just because you paid money, you're not assured of landing fish. You'll still need to apply considerable skill and thought to catch fish from these waters. All the following waters have been in operation for a number of years, and each is unique and worth the money. Call in advance for reservations, information, and conditions. Here's basic information you'll need to fly fish at these private waters. Check with the booking agent to get additional information about tackle, hatches, and any food or gear you may need.

Types of Fish

Rainbow, brown, and brook trout; bass; and bluegill.

Known Hatches

Varied.

Equipment to Use

Rods: 4–7 weight, 8–9½ feet in length.
Reels: Standard trout reels are fine.
Lines: Floating, full sink intermediate to type 4.
Leaders: 3X to 6X, 6–15 feet in length.
Wading: Most of these waters have wadable shorelines. Take a float tube if that's your preferred method of fishing still waters.

Flies to Use

Dries: Adult Damsel, Suspended Midge, Callibaetis Parachute & Spinner, Elk Hair and Slow Water Caddis, Timberline Emerger, Griffith's Gnat, Palomino, Century Drive Midge, Comparadun, Light Cahill.
Nymphs: Scud, Damsel, Dragonfly, Midge, Snail, Gold Ribbed Hare's Ear, Pheasant Tail, Bird's Nest, Soft Hackle, Prince, Zug Bug, Tied-Down Caddis, Carey Special, Cates Turkey, Water Boatman.
Streamers: Woolly Bugger, Zonker, Matuka, Leech Patterns.

When to Fish

Consult the booking agents for the private "season" and the best times to fish.

Accommodations & Services

Some, variable, or none! Ask.

Rating

You'd have to rate these lakes at 7 or better.

1. Antoine Ranch

Located 65 miles east of Prineville, the ranch has 40,000 acres of private timber-covered slopes, steep draws, and grass-covered plateaus. Angler numbers are limited weekly. Anglers have access to six lakes offering trophy rainbow trout. Day fishing and guided fishing packages available. Cabins and meals included. Contact Go West Outfitters, (541) 447-4082, The Fly Box, (541) 388-3330.

2. Barnes Butte

Just outside the town of Prineville, Barnes offers bass, bluegill, and Kamloops trout. Mixing different techniques for the varied species can be fun (referred to as The Barnes Butte Grand Slam). Trout fishing is good all year. Bass and bluegill are more active in warm weather. Float tubing is popular, but a small boat (with an electric motor) is also a good way to fish. Contact Roger Hudspeth (541) 480-0791.

3. Bear Creek Lake

This 35-acre lake, about 60 miles east of Bend, is rich in aquatic life, especially damselflies and dragonflies. Also bring Water Boatmen, Leeches, Snails, scuds, and midges. Rainbows average 16 to 18 inches, but be prepared for the big tug from 5–7 pounders. Fishing is best from mid-April through early summer and again in late fall. At 4,600 feet, cool water keeps fishing consistent. Day trips are available for two to six anglers, or rent a cabin for groups staying overnight. Contact The Fly Box (541) 388-3330.

4. Buckhorn Ranch

About 20 minutes east of Sisters, this 15-acre lake offers one of the best and most easily accessed opportunities to catch and release *big* Kamloops and rainbow trout. The lake is full of damselflies, dragonflies, and caddis and is surrounded by hundreds of acres of farms and pasture land. Cover and rock outcroppings are plentiful. Casting from the bank is easy but a float tube is the best way to fish Buckhorn. Fish from March through July, or September through December. Day trips only. (877) 904-8341 or (541) 280-3669.

5. Lake of the Dunes

Located near Summer Lake, about 75 miles southeast of La Pine, these four lakes range in size from four to six acres. All hold trophy rainbow trout that will test your skills. Two large artesian wells feed the lakes with cold water. A rustic log cabin on site sleeps five and can be rented for overnight stays. Fly fishing only, March 1 to October 31. This is one of the better fly fishing bargains east of the Cascades. Contact The Patient Angler, (541) 389-6208.

6. Grindstone

Eighty miles east of Prineville and about 15 miles east of the town of Paulina, this ranch is in a magnificent high desert setting. It has been remodeled recently and is under new management. Five lakes, rich with scuds, leeches, and snails, hold trophy rainbow trout. Trout get "shoulders" here and fight hard. Multiday packages include lodging and food. Bring a float tube to access the best fishing. Guides on the property can show you the waters and help with techniques. Contact Roger Carbone, (541) 416-9191. www.grindstonelakes.com, www.carbonesflyfishing.com.

7. Summer Lake Inn

This inn, southeast of La Pine on Highway 31, has a large pond stocked with trout, bass, and bluegill. Guests staying at the bed and breakfast–style inn can fish for free. Contact Darrell Seven, (800) 261-2778.

8. Long Hollow Ranch

Long Hollow Ranch offers fine still-water fly fishing about 20 minutes from Sisters, near the Lower Bridge section of the Deschutes River. The five lakes on the ranch are in pastures and up against desert rim rocks. All waters hold rainbow and brown trout, and you can fish from the shore or from float tubes or pontoons. An exciting feature here is stalking large fish and sight fishing from the banks. Lunch at the ranch house is provided. Open from March through October. Contact The Fly Fisher's Place, (541) 549-3474.

9. Wild Billy Lake

A 200-acre lake close to Klamath Falls features fly fishing only; game fish include big Kamloops and Mt. Lassen rainbows and Donaldson steelhead (up to 14 pounds). Float tubing is the most popular way to fish. Small boats (no gas motors) are allowed. There are picnic tables and campsites at the lake, or you can rent a small cabin. A motel and restaurant are within driving distance. Contact Ron Thienes, (541) 747-5595, Sunriver Fly Shop, (541) 593-8814.

10. Wild Winds Ranch & Justinson's Ranch

These properties are very near each other in high desert habitat near the town of Grass Valley. Both ranches have lakes full of rainbow and Kamloops trout. Wild Winds has three lakes. Justinson's Ranch has 24 still waters and lots of room. Contact The Fly Box, (541) 388-3330.

11. Alder Creek Ranch

This lake is very near Sisters, on the Cyrus Ranch. The area is landscaped, the lake has a small dock, and the fishing is very good for rainbow trout. Contact The Fly Fisher's Place, (541) 549-3474.

Resources

Western Oregon

The Caddis Fly Angling Shop
168 W Sixth Ave
Eugene, OR 97401
(541) 342-7005
www.thecaddisfly.com

Country Sport
126 SW First Ave
Portland, OR 97201
(503) 221-4545
www.csport.com

Creekside Fly Fishing
345 High St SE
Salem, OR 97301
(503) 588-1768
www.creeksideflyfishing.com

Fisherman's Marine & Outdoor
1120 N Hayden Meadows Drive
Portland, OR 97217-7546
(503) 283-0044
www.fishermans-marine.com

Fisherman's Marine & Outdoor
1900 SE McLoughlin Blvd
Oregon City, OR 97045
(503) 557-3313

Fly Country Outfitters
2157 Broadview Ct NW
Salem, OR 97304
(503) 581-8736
www.flycountry.com

The Fly Fishing Shop
PO Box 368
67296 E Hwy 26
Welches, OR 97067
(503) 622-4607
(800) 266-3971
www.flyfishusa.com

Home Waters Fly Fishing
444 W 3rd Ave
Eugene, OR 97401
(541) 342-6691

Kaufmann's Streamborn
8861 SW Commercial
Tigard, OR 97223
(503) 639-6400
www.kman.com

Northwest Fly Fishing Outfitters
10910 NE Halsey
Portland, OR 97220
(503) 252-1529

Northwest Outdoors Supply
435 SE Jackson St
Roseburg, OR 97470
(541) 440-3042

Oscar's Sporting Goods
380 SW 15th St
Madras, OR 97741
(541) 475-2962

The Scarlet Ibis Fly Shop
121 SW 4th St
Corvallis, OR 97333
(541) 754-1544
www.scarletibisflyshop.com

Central Oregon

Camp Sherman Store
25451 Forest Service Rd
Camp Sherman, OR 97730
(541) 595-6711
www.campshermanstore.com

Cascade Guides and Outfitters
Sunriver Village Mall, Bldg 21
Sunriver, OR 97707
(541) 593-2358

Central Oregon Outdoors
1935 S Hwy 97
Redmond, OR 97756
(541) 504-0372
www.centraloregonoutdoors.com

Deschutes Canyon Fly Shop
PO Box 334
599 S Hwy 197
Maupin, OR 97037
(541) 395-2565
www.flyfishingdeschutes.com

Deschutes River Outfitters
61115 S Hwy 97
Bend, OR 97702
(541) 388-8191
(800) 315-7272
www.deschutesoutfitters.com

Fin & Feather Fly Shop
785 NW 3rd St
Prineville, OR 97754-1430
(541) 447-8691

Fly & Field Outfitters
143A SW Century Dr
Bend, OR 97702
(541) 318-1616
www.flyandfield.com

Numb-Butt Fly Company
547 NE Bellevue Dr. Suite 201
Bend, OR 97701
(541) 330-6376
(888) 248-8309
www.numb-butt.com

The Fly Box Outfitters
1255 NE 3rd St
Bend, OR 97701
(541) 388-3330
(800) 411-3330
www.theflyboxoutfitters.com

The Fly Fisher's Place
151 W Main St
PO Box 1179
Sisters, OR 97759
(541) 549-3474
www.flyfishersplace.com

The Hook Fly Shop
Sunriver Village Mall, #21
PO Box 3676
Sunriver, OR 97707
(541) 593-2358
(888) 230-4665
www.cascadeguides.com

The Oasis
609 Hwy 197 S
Maupin, OR 97037
(541) 395-2611
www.deschutesriveroasis.com

The Patient Angler
55 NW Wall St
Bend, OR 97701
(541) 389-6208

Prineville Sporting Goods
346 N Deer St
Prineville, OR 97754
(541) 447-6883

Sunriver Fly Shop
56805 Venture Ln
PO Box 3511
Sunriver, OR 97707
(541) 593-8814
www.sunriverflyshop.com

Trophy Waters
101 S Grape St
Medford, OR 97501
(541) 734-2278
Fax: (541) 734-9700
www.trophywaters.net

Eastern Oregon

B & B Sporting Goods
Hwy 20 & W Conley
Hines, OR 97738
(541) 573-6200

Four Seasons Fly Shoppe
10210 Wallowa Lake Hwy
La Grande, OR 97850-8713
(541) 963-8420

High-desert trout fishing in the scenic canyon of the Lower Deschutes River. Photo by Brian O'Keefe.

Joseph Fly Shoppe
203 N Main St
Joseph, OR 97846
(541) 432-4343

Other Helpful Fly Shops

Bill Mason Sun Valley Outfitters
Sun Valley Mall
Sun Valley, ID 83353
(208) 622-9305
www.billmasonoutfitters.com

The Fly Shop
4140 Churn Creek Road
Redding, CA 96002
(800) 669-3474
www.theflyshop.com

Reno Fly Shop
294 E Moana Ln #14
Reno, NV 89502
(775) 825-3474
www.renoflyshop.com

Clubs & Associations

Angler's Club of Portland
PO Box 9235
Portland, OR 97207

California Trout
870 Market St, #528
San Francisco, CA 94102
(415) 392-8887
Fax: (415) 392-8895
www.caltrout.org

Cascade Family Fly Fishers
PO Box 5384
Eugene, OR 97705
www.cascadefamilyflyfishers.com

Central Oregon Fly Fishers
PO Box 1126
Bend, OR 97709
(541) 617-8837
www.coflyfishers.org

Clackamas Fly Fishers
PO Box 268
West Linn, OR 97068

Columbia Gorge Fly Fishers
1220 Methodist Rd
Hood River, OR 97058
http://community-gorge.net/cgflyfishers

Federation of Fly Fishers
National Headquarters
PO Box 1595
Bozeman, MT 59771
(460) 585-7592
www.fedflyfishers.org

IGFA – International Game Fish Association
Headquarters
300 Gulf Stream Way
Dania Beach, Florida 33004
(954) 927-2628
Fax (954) 924-4299
E-Mail: hq@igfa.org
www.igfa.org

Klamath County Fly Casters
PO Box 324
Klamath Falls, OR 97601

Lower Umpqua Fly Fishers
PO Box 521
Reedsport, OR 97467
http://lower-umpqua-flycasters.org

Mckenzie Fly Fishers
PO Box 10865
Eugene, OR 97440-2865
http://mckenzieflyfisher.org

Mid-Willamette Fly Fishers
PO Box 22
Corvallis, OR 97339

National Fresh Water Fishing Hall of Fame
PO Box 690
Hayward, WI 54843
(715) 634-4440
www.freshwater-fishing.org

Northwest Fly Fishers
PO Box 656
Troutdale, OR 97060

Oregon Council Federation of Fly Fishers
PO Box 2417
Grant's Pass, OR 97528
(541) 479-0009
www.oregonfff.org

Rainland Flycasters
PO Box 1045
Astoria, OR 97103
www.rainlandflycasters.homestead.com

Rogue Fly Fishers
PO Box 4637
Medford, OR 97501
www.rogueflyfishers.org

Santiam Fly Casters, Inc.
PO Box 691
Salem, OR 97308
www.santiamflycasters.com

The Steamboaters
PO Box 176
Idleyld Park, OR 97447
www.steamboaters.org

Sunriver Anglers
PO Box 4237
Sunriver, OR 97707

Government Resources

BLM - Bureau of Land Management
Oregon State Office
PO Box 2965
Portland, OR 97208
(503) 808-6002
Fax (503) 808-6308
www.or.blm.gov/index.htm

BLM Burns District
28910 Hwy 20
Hines, OR 97738
(541) 573-4400
Fax (541) 573-4411
www.or.blm.gov/index.htm

BLM Map Distribution Unit
PO Box 97208
Portland, OR 97208
(503) 808-6001
Fax (503) 808-6308
www.or.blm.gov/index.htm

ODFW - Oregon Department of Fish and Wildlife
Headquarters
3406 Cherry Ave NE
Salem, OR 97303
(503) 947-6000
(800) 720-6339
www.dfw.state.or.us/

ODFW Central
61374 Parrell Rd
Bend, OR 97702
(541) 388-6363

ODFW Malheur Watershed District
237 S Hines Blvd
Hines, OR 97738
(541) 573-6582

ODFW The Dalles
3561 Klindt Dr
The Dalles, OR 97058
(541) 296-8026

ODFW John Day
PO Box 9
John Day, OR 97845
(541) 575-1167

ODFW Klamath Falls
1850 Miller Island Rd
Klamath Falls, OR 97603
(541) 883-5732

ODFW Lakeview
101 N "D" St
Lakeview, OR 97630
(541) 947-2950

Mt. Jefferson looks down on the Metolius River near Camp Sherman, Oregon. Photo by Brian O'Keefe.

ODFW Madras
1950 NW Mill St
Madras, OR 97741
(541) 475-2183

ODFW Ontario
3814 Clark Blvd
Ontario, OR 97914
(541) 889-6975

ODFW Prineville
2042 SE Paulina Hwy
Prineville, OR 97754
(541) 447-5111

Oregon Department of Transportation
(541) 378-6254
(888) 275-6368
www.odot.state.or.us/home/

Oregon Tourism Commission
Salem, OR 97310
(503) 986-0000
Fax (503) 986-0001
www.traveloregon.com

Warm Springs Indian Reservation
PO Box C
Warm Springs, OR 97761
(541) 553-1161
http://extension.oregonstate.edu/warmsprings/wscom.htm

Forest Services

Deschutes National Forest
1645 Hwy 20 E
Bend, OR 97701
(541) 383-5300
www.fs.fed.us/r6/

Malheur National Forest
431 Patterson Bridge Rd
John Day, OR 97845
(541) 515-1731
www.fs.fed.us/r6/

Ochoco National Forest
3160 NE 3rd St
Prineville, OR 97741
(541) 416-6500
www.fs.fed.us/r6/

Oregon Department of Forestry
2600 State St
Salem, OR 97310
(503) 945-7200
www.odf.state.or.us/

Oregon State Parks Camping
(800) 452-5687
www.prd.state.or.us/

USDA Forest Service
Pacific North West Region
PO Box 3623
Portland, OR 97208
(503) 808-2468
www.fs.fed.us/r6/

USDA Forest Service
National Headquarters
1400 Independence Ave SW
Washington, D.C. 20250-0002
(202) 205-8333
www.fs.fed.us/recreation/map/finder.shtml

Winema National Forest
2819 Dahlia St
Klamath, OR 97601
(541) 883-6714

References & Other Reading Material

Caddisflies
Gary LaFontaine

Fishing in Oregon
Casali & Diness

Fishing Oregon's Deschutes River
Scott Richmond

Hatch Guide for Western Lakes
Jim Schollmeyer

Hatch Guide to Western Streams
Jim Schollmeyer

Mayflies
Malcolm Knopp & Robert Cornier

Oregon Sport Fishing Regulations
ODFW

Oregon Atlas and Gazetteer
Delorme Mapping

Western Hatches
Rick Hafele & Dave Hughes

Fly Fishing The Internet

http://gorp.away.com
www.amrivers.org
www.fbn-flyfish.com
www.fedflyfishers.org
www.fly-fishing-women.com
www.flyfish.com
www.flyfishamerica.com
www.flyfishing.com
www.flyshop.com
www.gofishing.com
www.gssafaris.com
www.ohwy.com
www.tu.org

Directories

www.fish-world.com

Knots

www.earlham.edu (search for "knots")
www.fishnmap.com
www.maps4u.com/news/2001Aug/GPSClasses.html

Guidebooks

www.amazon.com
www.barnesandnoble.com
www.powells.com

Travel Agents

www.expedia.com
www.orbitz.com
www.travelweb.com
www.travelocity.com

Air Travel

Alaska
www.alaskaair.com
(800) 426-0333

American
www.aa.com
(800) 433-7300

America West
www.americawest.com
(800) 235-9292

Continental
www.continental.com
(800) 525-0280

Delta
www.delta.com
(800) 221-1212

Northwest
www.nwa.com
(800) 225-2525

Southwest
www.southwest.com
(800) 435-9792

United
www.united.com
(800) 241-6522

US Airways
www.usair.com
(800) 428-4322

: angler scouts the Crooked River on a brisk winter day.
oto by Brian O'Keefe.

Conservation

No Nonsense Fly Fishing Guidebooks believes that, in addition to local information and gear, fly fishers need clean water and healthy fish. We encourage preservation, improvement, conservation, enjoyment and understanding of our waters and their inhabitants. While fly fishing, take care of the place, practice catch and release and try to avoid spawning fish.

When you aren't fly fishing, a good way to help all things wild and aquatic is to support organizations dedicated to these ideas. We encourage you to get involved, learn more and to join such organizations.

American Fly Fishing Trade Association .... (360) 636-0708
American Rivers .... (202) 347-7550
California Trout .... (415) 392-8887
Deschutes Basin Land Trust .... (541) 330-0017
Ducks Unlimited .... (800) 453-8257
Federation of Fly Fishers .... (406) 585-7592
International Game Fish Association .... (954) 927-2628
International Women Fly Fishers .... (925) 934-2461
New Mexico Trout .... (505) 884-5262
Oregon Trout .... (503) 222-9091
Outdoor Writers Association of America .... (406) 728-7434
Recreational Fishing Alliance .... (888) JOIN-RFA
Rails-to-Trails Conservancy .... (202) 331-9696
Theodore Roosevelt Conservation Partnership .... (877) 770-8722
Trout Unlimited .... (800) 834-2419

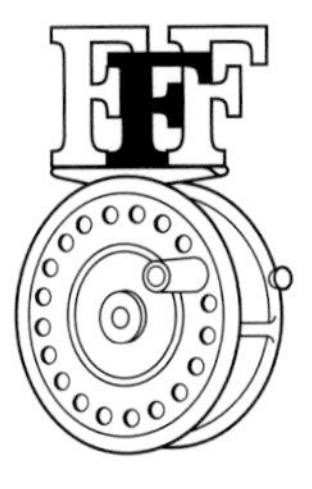

A triumphant steelheader and his catch on the Lower Deschutes River. Photo by Brian O'Keefe.

Find Your Way with These No Nonsense Guides

Fly Fishing Colorado
Jackson Streit

Your experienced guide gives you the quick, clear understanding of the essential information you'll need to fly fish Colorado's most outstanding waters. Use this book to plan your Colorado fly fishing trip, and take this guide along for ready reference. This popular guide has been updated, redesigned and is in its third printing.
ISBN #1-892469-13-8 .... $19.95

Fly Fishing New Mexico
Taylor Streit

Since 1970, Mr. Streit has been New Mexico's foremost fly fishing authority and professional guide. He's developed many fly patterns used throughout the region. Taylor owned the Taos Fly Shop for ten years and managed a bone fishing lodge in the Bahamas. He makes winter fly fishing pilgrimages to Argentina where he escorts fly fishers and explorers. Newly revised.
ISBN #1-892469-04-9 .... $18.95

Fly Fishing Arizona
Glenn Tinnin

Desert, forest, lava fields, red rocks and canyons. Here is where to go and how to fish 32 streams, lakes, bass waters, reservoirs in Arizona. Newly revised.
ISBN #1-892469-02-2 .... $18.95

Fly Fishing Southern Baja
Gary Graham

With this book you can fly to Baja, rent a car and go out on your own to find exciting saltwater fly fishing! Mexico's Baja Peninsula is now one of the premier destinations for saltwater fly anglers. Newly revised.
ISBN #1-892469-00-6 .... $18.95

Fly Fishing California
Ken Hanley

Coming Soon: Mr. Hanley and some very talented contributors like Jeff Solis, Dave Stanley, Katie Howe and others, have fly fished nearly every top water in California. Saltwater, bass, steelhead, high mountains, they provide all you need to discover the best places to fly fish in the Golden State. Coming soon, newly revised.
ISBN #1-892469-10-3 .... $19.95

Fly Fishing Nevada
Dave Stanley

The Truckee, Walker, Carson, Eagle, Davis, Ruby, mountain lakes and more. Mr. Stanley is recognized nationwide as the most knowledgeable fly fisher and outdoorsman in the state of Nevada. He owns and operates the Reno Fly Shop and Truckee River Outfitters in Truckee, California. Coming soon, newly revised.
ISBN #0-9637256-2-9 .... $18.95

Fly Fishing Utah
Steve Schmidt

Utah yields extraordinary, uncrowded and little known fishing. Steve Schmidt, outfitter and owner of Western Rivers Fly Shop in Salt Lake City has explored these waters for over 28 years. Covers mountain streams and lakes, tailwaters, bass waters and reservoirs. Coming soon, newly revised.
ISBN #0-9637256-8-8 .... $19.95

Fly Fishing Idaho
Bill Mason

The Henry's Fork, Salmon, Snake and Silver Creek plus 24 other waters. Mr. Mason penned the first fly fishing guidebook to Idaho in 1994. It was updated in 1996 and showcases Bill's 30 plus years of Idaho fly fishing. Coming soon, newly revised.
ISBN #0-9637256-1-0 .... $14.95

A Woman's Guide To Fly Fishing Favorite Waters
Yvonne Graham

Forty-five of the top women fly fishing experts reveal their favorite waters. From scenic spring creeks in the East, big trout waters in the Rockies to exciting Baja: all described from the female perspective. A major donation goes to Casting for Recovery, a nonprofit organization for women recovering from breast cancer.

ISBN #1-892469-03-0 .... $19.95

Business Traveler's Guide To Fly Fishing The Western States
Bob Zeller

A seasoned road warrior reveals where one can fly fish within a two hour drive of every major airport in thirteen western states. Don't miss another day fishing!

ISBN #1-892469-01-4 .... $18.95

Fly Fishing Magdalena Bay
Gary Graham

Guide and excursion leader Gary Graham (Baja On The Fly) lays out the truth about fly fishing for snook in mangroves, and off-shore marlin. Photos, illustrations, maps, and travel information, this is "the Bible" for this unique region.

ISBN #1-892469-08-1 .... $24.95

Fly Fishing Pyramid Lake Nevada
Terry Barron

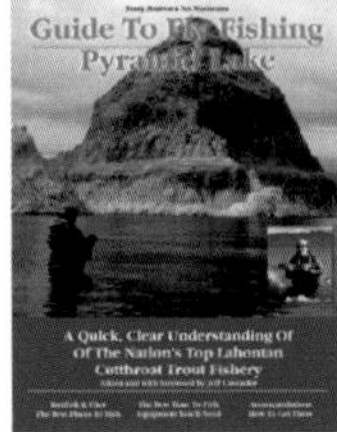

The Gem of the Desert is full of huge Lahontan Cutthroat trout. Terry has recorded everything you need to fly fish the most outstanding trophy cutthroat fishery in the U.S. Where else can you get tired of catching 18-25" trout?

ISBN #0-9637256-3-7 .... $15.95

Fly Fishing Lee's Ferry
Dave Foster

This guide provides a clear understanding of the complex and fascinating 15 miles of river that can provide fly anglers 40-fish days. Detailed maps direct fly and spin fishing access. Learn about history, boating and geology, the area's beauty. Indispensable for the angler and intrepid visitor to the Marble Canyon.

ISBN #1-892469-07-3 .... $21.95

Seasons of the Metolius
John Judy

This book describes how a beautiful riparian environment both changes and stays the same over the years. This look at nature comes from a man who makes his living working in nature and chronicles John Judy's 30 years of study, writing and fly fishing his beloved home water, the crystal clear Metolius River in central Oregon.

ISBN #1-892469-11-1 .... $20.95

Where No Nonsense Guides Come From

No Nonsense guidebooks give you a quick, clear understanding of the essential information needed to fly fish a region's most outstanding waters. The authors are highly experienced and qualified local fly fishers. Maps are tidy versions of the author's sketchess. These guides are produced by the fly fishers, their friends, and spouses of fly fishers, at No Nonsense Fly Fishing Guidebooks.

All who produce No Nonsense guides believe in providing top quality products at a reasonable price. We also believe all information should be verified. We never hesitate to go out, fly rod in hand, to verify the facts and figures that appear in the pages of these guides. The staff is committed to this research.

It's dirty work, but we're glad to do it for you.

Dramatic desert vistas like this are a constant companion on the Owyhee River.
Photo by Matt Johnson.

Fly Fishing Knots

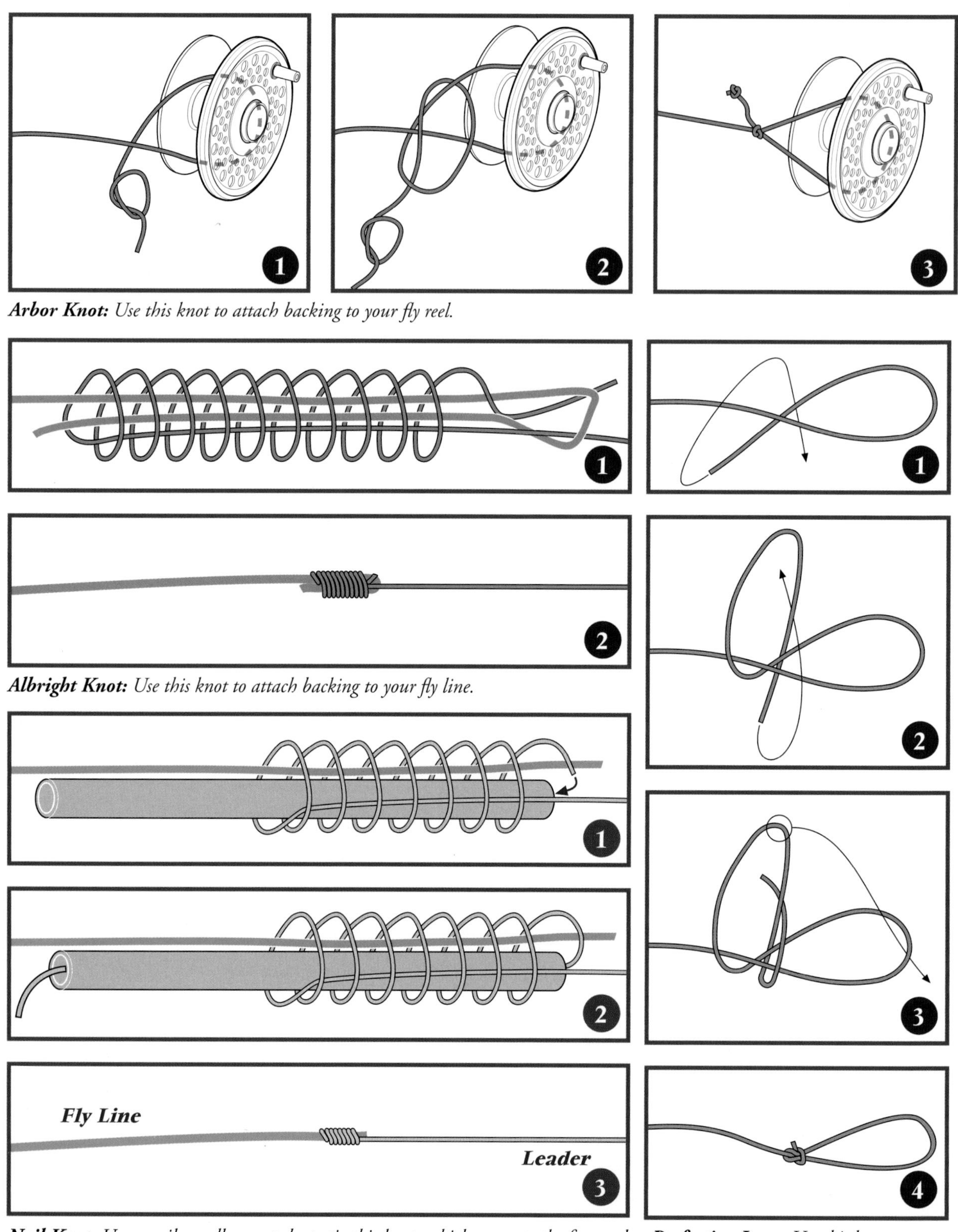

Arbor Knot: *Use this knot to attach backing to your fly reel.*

Albright Knot: *Use this knot to attach backing to your fly line.*

Nail Knot: *Use a nail, needle or a tube to tie this knot, which connects the forward end of the fly line to the butt end of the leader. Follow this with a Perfection Loop and you've got a permanent end loop that allows easy leader changes.*

Perfection Loop: *Use this knot to create a loop in the butt end of the leader for loop-to-loop connections.*

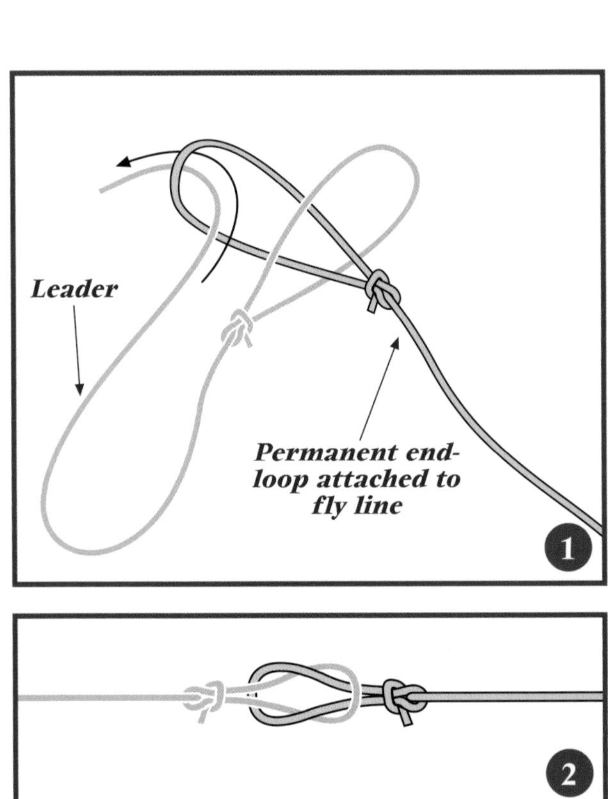

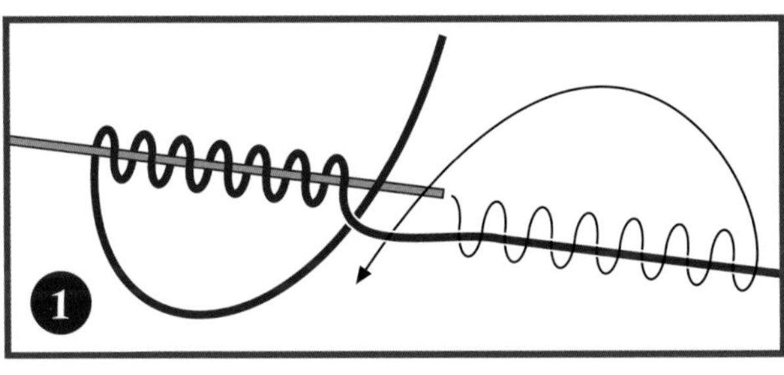

Loop-to-Loop: Easy connection of leader to a permanent monofilament end loop added to the tip of the fly line.

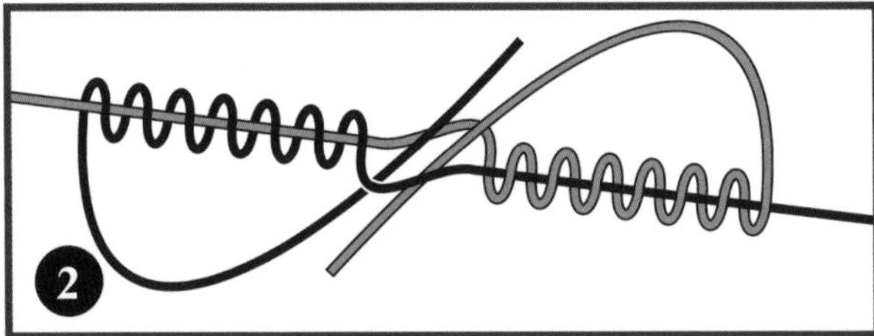

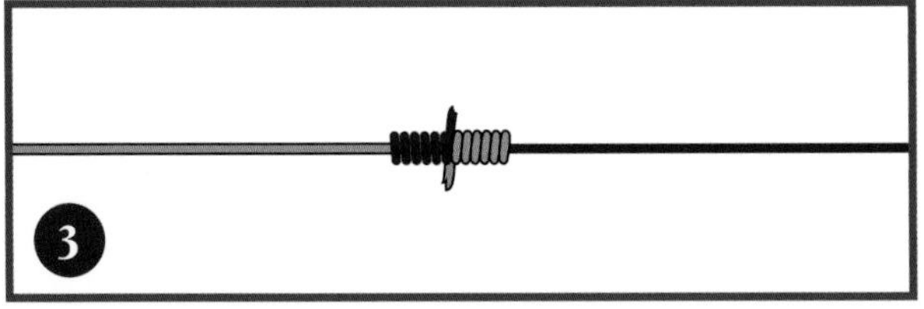

Blood Knot: *Use this knot to connect sections of leader tippet material. Hard to tie, but worth the effort.*

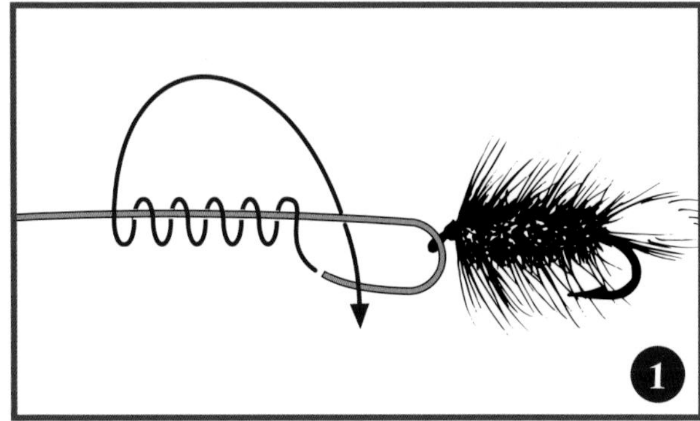

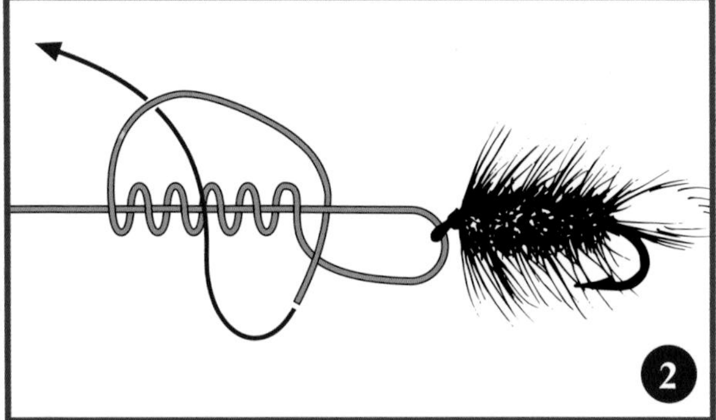

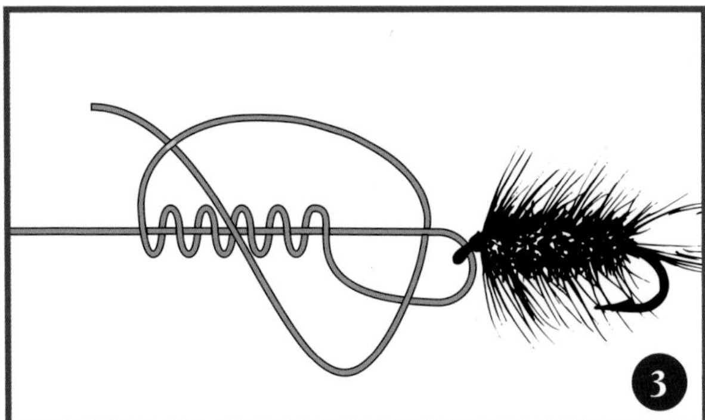

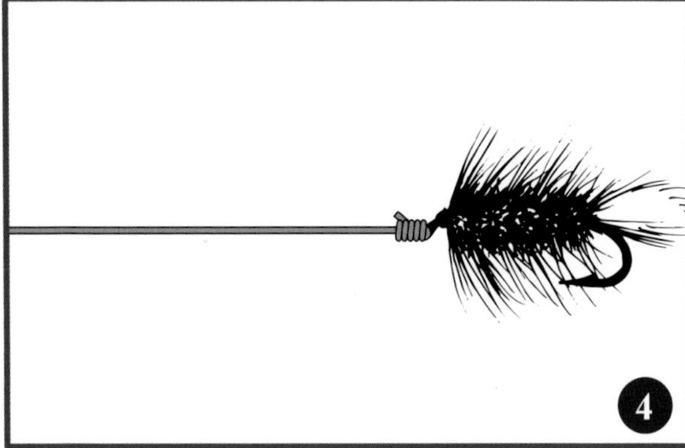

Improved Clinch Knot: *Use this knot to attach the fly to the end of the tippet. Remember to moisten the knot before pulling it up tight.*

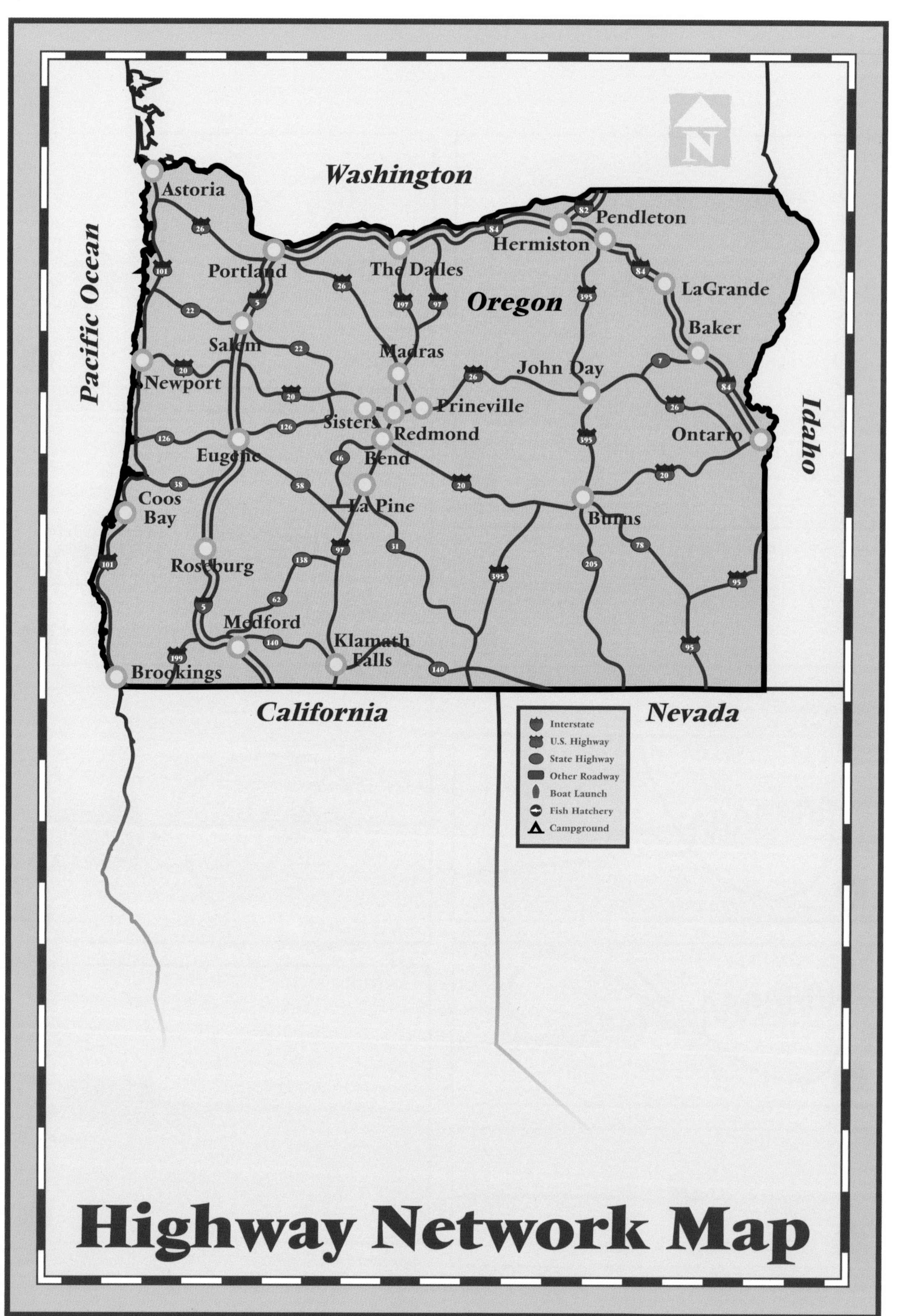

A small spring amidst stark desert environs near Summer Lake, Oregon serves as the source of the Ana River. Photo by Matt Johnson.

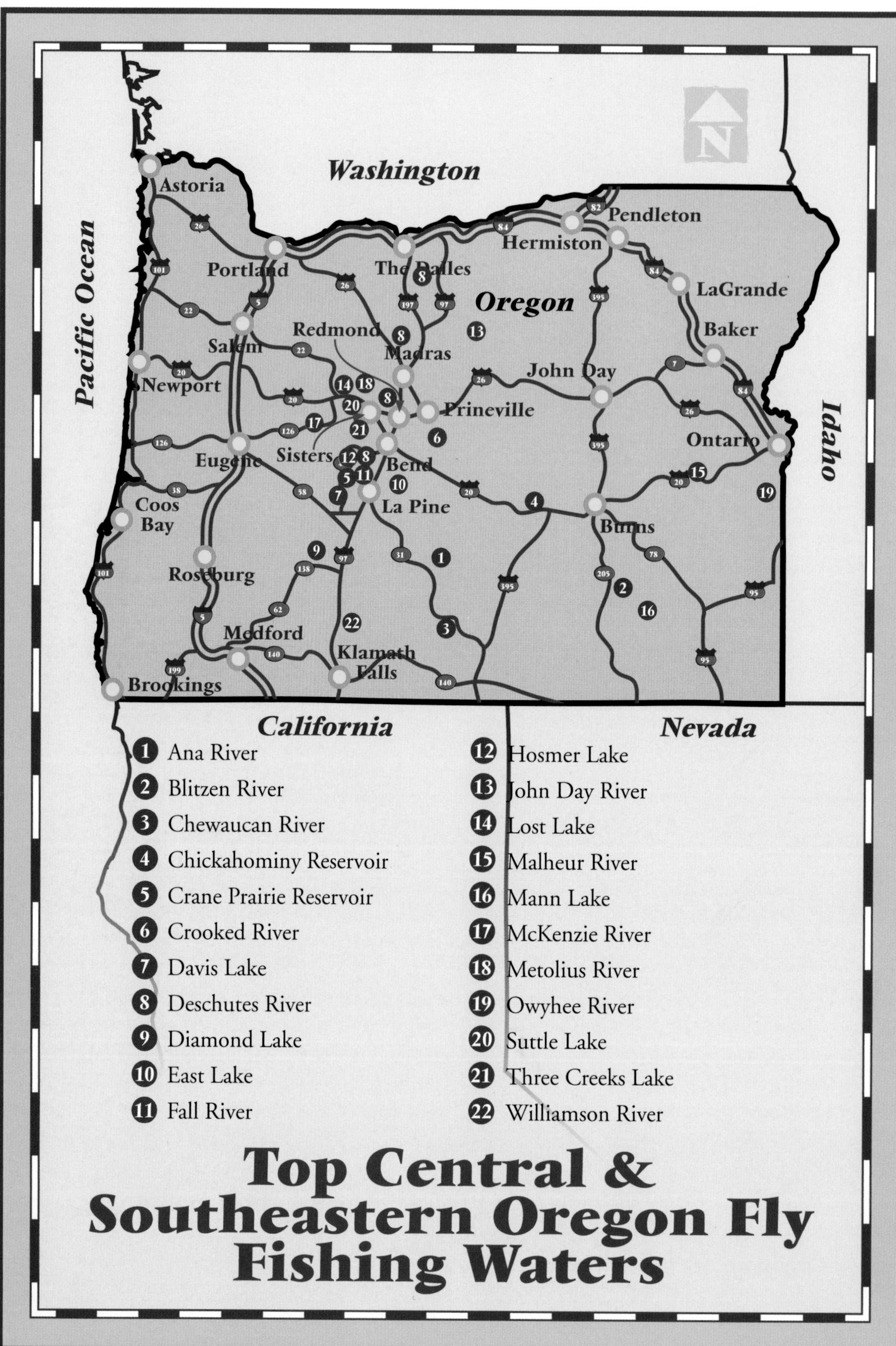
Washington
Pacific Ocean
Idaho
California
Nevada
Oregon
Astoria
Portland
The Dalles
Hermiston
Pendleton
LaGrande
Baker
Salem
Redmond
Madras
Newport
John Day
Prineville
Sisters
Bend
Eugene
Ontario
La Pine
Coos Bay
Burns
Roseburg
Medford
Klamath Falls
Brookings
1 Ana River
2 Blitzen River
3 Chewaucan River
4 Chickahominy Reservoir
5 Crane Prairie Reservoir
6 Crooked River
7 Davis Lake
8 Deschutes River
9 Diamond Lake
10 East Lake
11 Fall River
12 Hosmer Lake
13 John Day River
14 Lost Lake
15 Malheur River
16 Mann Lake
17 McKenzie River
18 Metolius River
19 Owyhee River
20 Suttle Lake
21 Three Creeks Lake
22 Williamson River
Top Central & Southeastern Oregon Fly Fishing Waters